"This leadership book is different. It focuses on the often-ignored ingredients of becoming a transformative leader—virtues. This includes the novel concept of loving the people you lead. Developing behaviors and actions grounded in the virtues set forth in this book is the key to achieving extraordinary organizational results."

—**RAY L. STEINMETZ**, projects executive, ExxonMobil (retired)

"Great lessons on virtuous leadership and teaming are captured here. If you want to be a difference-maker in your organization, read this book, commit to the virtues of leadership, align your actions, and develop great teams. It is a proven road map for continued success."

—**JOHN MAHONEY**, PMP, president/chief operating officer, High Expectations International, LLC

"My entire team utilizes the five virtues daily. Having a common language about leadership and how to support our internal and external customers has made us an even stronger marketing organization."

—**LISA DATKA**, chief marketing officer, Early Learning Academies

"Whether you are a new team leader or an experienced executive who has been leading teams for years, *The Virtue Proposition* will speak to your soul. With his wit and inspirational stories, Berg unlocks the essence of what every leader CAN and MUST DO in a world that so desperately needs courageous leaders who step up. Virtue Intelligence is the key!"

—**JULIE CAMPBELL**, president and CEO, Severn Leadership Group

"*The Virtue Proposition*, thoroughly researched and thoughtfully written, provides an intriguing new way of looking at leadership: through the lens of virtues. With love, integrity, truth, excellence, and relationships (LITER), Berg puts forward five timeless virtues that address the current crisis in leadership, from boardrooms to politics. Backed by strong research and drawing on an impressive leadership track record of the author, this book provides both thoughtful analysis and inspiration for change on the reader's part. Read this book, embrace a new kind of virtues-driven leadership, and become a true changemaker!"
—URS KOENIG, founder, Radical Humility Leadership Institute; former UN peacekeeper; and author of *Radical Humility: Be a Badass Leader AND a Good Human*

"To read Sig's *The Virtue Proposition* is to gain an insight into a lifetime of leadership rooted in love and courage. It's a book that inspires a virtues-based approach, with personal stories and practical guidance of how to live and lead in a virtuous way. At a moment in time when moral and egoless leadership is so greatly needed, Sig takes a seemingly old-fashioned concept of character and brings it to life as something real and necessary by framing it in terms of enduring, transcendent virtues. It is a book and a message that I dearly wish I had read as I started out almost thirty-five years ago, both in terms of how I am as a leader and what I should expect from the people who lead me."
—MICHELLE QUEST GILLIS, partner of KPMG in UK (retired)

"In every leadership sphere, virtues must be prioritized and prevail. Sig Berg takes a deep and inspiring dive into the provocative concept of virtue intelligence (VQ), a term that is too often overlooked but essential to lasting performance. Read this book to raise your VQ and help your team embrace a new level of excellence."

—**JOSH LINKNER**, two-time *New York Times* bestselling author, five-time tech entrepreneur, and managing partner, Mudita Venture Partners

"*The Virtue Proposition* is a much-needed, timely reflection on morally serious leadership. Sig Berg mines the riches of deeply rooted wisdom and highlights the singular place of virtue for leaders and teams that hope to excel in the midst of today's challenges and complexities. This book challenges our shallow conceptions of leadership and takes us on a remarkable journey of insight and inspiration."

—**DAN BRYANT**, executive vice president, Fortune Five, and former U.S. assistant attorney general

"A fresh and necessary approach to leadership and team building based on the understanding that 'leadership begins with you but is not about you.' In an age when many leaders are self-focused and leadership training is about 'how to do,' this book teaches a leader about 'how to BE.'"

—**STEDMAN GARBER**, oil service industry CEO (retired)

"The virtues-based leadership that Sig prescribes is only possible when your head and heart are aligned so your hands take action. When you teach your team that, you get more consistency, productivity, and greater purpose than you ever thought possible."

—**PAUL EPSTEIN**, former NFL and NBA executive, bestselling author of *Better Decisions Faster* and *The Power of Playing Offense*

"Leadership does not function in a vacuum. It must have an end. *The Virtue Proposition* reminds us that its aim is to serve something larger than yourself—especially a team. Since dense networks are the way things get accomplished, team-oriented virtues-based leaders are the key catalyst in making organizations and communities a reflection of our highest virtues. Few books are more timely and more needed today than *The Virtue Proposition*."

—**DAVID JOHN SEEL, JR.**, PhD, cultural impact and strategy specialist, and author of *Network Power: The Science of Making a Difference*

**www.amplifypublishinggroup.com**

*The Virtue Proposition: Five Virtues That Will Transform Leadership, Team Performance, and You*

**For more information, please contact:**
Amplify Publishing, an imprint of Amplify Publishing Group
620 Herndon Parkway, Suite 220
Herndon, VA 20170
info@amplifypublishing.com

Library of Congress Control Number: 2023922761

CPSIA Code: PRV0124A

ISBN-13: 979-8-89138-059-2

Printed in the United States

Hope is being able to see that
there is light despite all of the darkness.

ARCHBISHOP DESMOND TUTU
*Nobel Peace Prize Laureate*

# THE
# *VIRTUE*
# PROPOSITION

*Five Virtues That Will
Transform Leadership,
Team Performance, and You*

# Sig Berg

*Founder,* **Severn Leadership Group**

an imprint of Amplify Publishing Group

# CONTENTS

# *FOREWORD*

---

*The Virtue Proposition* is not just another leadership book—it's a rallying cry for leaders of today and tomorrow to embrace a profound shift in their approach. Sig Berg's journey has been marked by a relentless pursuit of excellence and integrity, and his insights have the power to transform how you think about leadership.

Sig and I have been grappling with the same types of issues for decades. In our roles as leaders and coaches, we've encountered countless leaders who face the complicated challenge of creating teams and companies rooted in integrity, honesty, and ethics. It's not just about individual growth; it's about creating a culture of integrity that becomes the foundation for everything their company does.

Sig's journey, from a nuclear engineer to a pastor, has provided him with a unique perspective on leadership that goes beyond the superficial values-based leadership we encounter today. He has experienced the high-stakes world of nuclear reactors and the solemn responsibility that comes with it, where there are no casual do-overs. In such environments, leadership on bald tires, rooted in values rather than virtues, is not an option—it's a recipe for disaster.

What sets Sig's work apart is his unwavering commitment to the idea that knowing why you, your team, and your organization pursue their goals is the key to realizing those goals and the difference they can make. This book insists that virtues lead the way, and it challenges the prevalent notion that values alone are enough. Sig emphasizes that before we can learn how to lead virtuously, we must understand why it matters. Only when leaders and teams fully grasp the purpose and performance that virtues bring, can they achieve and surpass their goals.

Leadership, as *The Virtue Proposition* underscores, is not just about achieving success; it's about leaving a lasting legacy of virtue and excellence. It's about making the world a better place through virtuous leadership, which combines transcendent virtues, emotional and virtue intelligence, and technical competence to enable organizations to reach their greatest potential as high performance teams.

I invite you to join this aspirational movement of virtuous leadership. As you delve into these pages, be prepared to reevaluate your understanding of leadership, to be inspired, and to embark on a collective pilgrimage toward performance excellence and a better world.

**Dr. Marshall Goldsmith**
*Thinkers50* #1 Executive Coach and *New York Times* bestselling author of *The Earned Life*, *Triggers*, and *What Got You Here Won't Get You There*

---

# CALLING ALL
# CHANGE-MAKERS

This book is for the inspired, the courageous, the change-makers.

These are the individuals who will deliver performance excellence, whether measured by return on investment, increased market share, rate of growth, employee retention, or any other metric. The promise of the book is this: virtuous leaders are the change-makers who inspire virtues-grounded teams that deliver consistent excellence. *The Virtue Proposition* explains how to achieve this. Know first that it will require courage. What is laid out here is not the path of traditional leadership, with its focus on the rules and rituals of boardrooms and c-suites. And it is not the path of iconoclastic leadership, which urges you to move fast and break things. Neither of these paths has, nor ever will, deliver consistent excellent performance. What is needed is a third way of leadership: virtue leadership.

What makes *The Virtue Proposition* transformational isn't just its how-to insights and strategies. *The Virtue Proposition* will inspire you, your team, and your organization for the better because it insists that before you learn how, you must know why.

Only virtuous leaders of virtues-grounded teams know fully why their purpose and performance matters, which immediately informs how they will achieve and surpass their goals. For a small business this might mean surviving year one. For an established company, this might mean exceeding the prior quarter's safety, profit, and production records. For a hospital system, this might mean lower costs per discharge, lower readmission rates, lower mortality rates. Goals are bottom-line results that in order to be realized sometimes demand you know why it matters that you and your team seek excellence.

I was chief engineer of the nuclear submarine USS Sunfish when, during a training exercise, we had a fire in the auxiliary compartment just forward of the Engine Room. We were under a sheet of extremely thick ice. Surfacing to clear and clean the air was out of the question. Our chief electrician, chief machinist mate, and I passed through the watertight door into the compartment filling with smoke. For the safety of the remaining crew and the vessel, for the integrity of the mission we'd all been tasked with, that door was sealed behind us. Either we solved the problem and walked out, or we would be carried out. The bottom line was: save the ship, save the crew, and complete the mission.

Because all three men who entered that compartment were animated by a dedication to a higher calling that turned a virtuous code of conduct into peak excellent performance, I lived to write this book.

This book holds to the unwavering commitment that knowing why you, your team, and your organization pursues its goals determines whether those goals are realized and, more importantly, the difference those goals will make. The greatest, most profound, and consequential difference you and your team can achieve requires letting virtues lead. Values matter, though how they matter depends entirely on what is being valued. When a team pursues a value proposition—a goal that promises to make a product, a company, an idea, or a person more appealing in the short term—they can discover that there are a thousand corners to cut, truths to bend, facts to ignore. When a team pursues a virtue proposition—a goal that promises to make a product, a company, an idea, or a person consistently better—they discover they have no such options.

To spy the difference ask yourself this: would you rather trust your family to a car designed and built by a team pursuing value propositions or virtue propositions? What about the building materials that go into your home, the ingredients that go into your food, the care that is provided at your nearest hospital?

Tragically, we live in a world filled with too many leaders, followers, and teams enthralled with short-term value propositions. And everywhere we look, we see the consequences.

It is appallingly apparent that there is a crisis among American leadership. It is a crisis of character. Lies, fraud, verbal coarseness, hypocrisy, greed, and affairs are both endemic and reaching epic proportions. Various forms of corruption are now expected behavior across every sphere of national life: politics, business, media, entertainment, sports, and religion. Something is terribly wrong. Paralleling this crisis is growing cynicism about leadership. The national news on cable TV is a daily soap opera of scandal. The pattern is to deflect with personal attacks, pointing the finger at one's opponents, avoiding accountability. Honest observers conclude that this is not a problem of the left or the right but a society-wide crisis across every sphere of social life witnessed most acutely among the nation's—indeed the world's—leaders.

We long for nobility, virtue, character, and altruism, yet find its opposite. We also long for truth, dependability, accountability, and pride-in-performance from service industries, product manufacturers, and the world's leaders, yet all too often find its opposite.

It can change; it must. It requires the inspired, the courageous, the change-makers to embrace the virtue proposition. It requires leaders to have technical competence and solid relational skills. However, those two components must be integrated with a crucial third element, often missing today, *virtue* intelligence (VQ). This core component embraces five timeless and transcendent virtues: love, integrity, truth, excellence, relationships (LITER), all catalyzed by courage. Integrated with emotional intelligence, *virtue* intelligence serves as an internal compass guiding a leader's life, decisions, and behavior. These *virtuous leaders* will become the leaders of virtuous teams that are then able to deliver superior results.

Leadership books abound. Leadership training is a growth industry. Yet few such books and training programs assume that character is an essential aspect of successful leadership apart from lip service. When the technical aspects of leadership are prioritized, as is common today, character becomes less and less important. But when the relational and organizational aspects of leadership are prioritized, character becomes essential. But here a deeper problem emerges.

When leadership books discuss character, it is discussed in terms of values and not virtues. The distinction is critical. The difference between the two is the heart of this book. When character is discussed in terms of values, character is framed in a manner that has little traction under pressure. Value-based leadership promotes leadership that entertains the possibility of cutting corners, bending truths, ignoring the facts. I call it leadership on bald tires. Under the complex pressures of modern life these bald tires do not keep the car on the road. This is what we are witnessing today among America's senior leadership.

Like the passengers in a car on bald tires, the followers of our current leaders run the risk of suffering the consequences of the weaknesses of their leaders.

In the fall of 2022, Oxford University's Jubilee Centre for Character and Virtue held their 10th Anniversary conference at Oriel College on the theme "Integrating Research on Character and Virtue." At the final celebratory dinner, Dr. James Rahn of the Kern Family Foundation gave an address challenging the distinguished attendees that after ten years of focused effort their work was not sufficient.[1] History demonstrates, Rahn warned, that we "must take to heart the warning of University of Virginia sociologist James Davison Hunter, 'We want character but without unyielding convictions, we want strong morality but without the emotional burdens of guilt or shame, we want virtue but without moral justifications that invariably offend; we want good without having to name evil; we want decency without the authority to insist upon it; we want moral community without any limitations to personal freedom. In short, we want what we cannot possibly have on the terms that we want it.'"[2]

Eventually, what we want and what we need is not a matter of preference but a matter of essential performance. And when peak performance is essential, leaders and teams armed with technical competence and committed to the virtue proposition give rise to something remarkable: belief in a common commitment to a shared purpose that transcends any single individual.

When I first reported to the Sunfish, the captain ordered me to his stateroom where he was direct and transparent. Everything that happened on that ship was his responsibility, everything, which included me. But everything that fell under my responsibilities as chief engineer was mine. The message was plain. Screw ups under my watch were mine, and my screw ups became his. The captain then spelled out how he'd manage this. He would trust me to do my job, only occasionally "pulling the string, seeing what came up." Like a fisherman checking his lines, he'd pull a string, and if nothing came up, everything continued as usual. If something did come up—a personnel problem, a lapse in procedure, an ignored detail—it became his responsibility to step into my responsibilities. Unsaid was what every submariner knows: the integrity of the hull and nuclear reactor, the integrity of the mission, the integrity of each crew member's life depended on the personal integrity of all on board to do their job to the highest standards of excellence as possible.

Everyone on the Sunfish lived with daily reminders of the necessity of dependable character, and on some days were asked to demonstrate it to the extreme.

On entering that smoke-filling compartment, from the moment the chief electrician and the chief machinist mate and

I put on our emergency breathing masks until the moment we walked back out that once-sealed compartment, our training, our wordless familiarity with what had to happen and in what order, and our implicit trust in each other took over. We did our jobs as if we were one. The bottom-line results were lives saved: mission maintained.

So many today want character in leadership but without the constraint of virtue. You can't. It is not just that such virtues-less character is insufficient to the moral challenges of our time, such morality is insufficient for leadership. Effective team leadership demands more.

Few business leaders understand the distinction between values and virtues. In common parlance they are often used interchangeably. But they mean very different things and in practice lead to very different results. Many companies select a set of values which organize their work and define their brand, but these corporate values in turn need to be grounded in transcendent virtues. This happens when those virtues are demonstrated in the character and conduct of corporate leaders. Absent that, neither virtues nor values will ever gain sufficient leverage and traction within their organization.

Blurring the difference between values and virtues is a common and increasingly fatal error.

Values are moral sentiments rooted in expressive individualism. They are a choice that an individual makes about moral priorities based on their feelings. Three things are characteristic of values: they are the result of individual choice, they are based in the subjectivity of the self and feelings, and they are malleable over time and place. Values amount to little more than individual opinion. It is not uncommon for leadership programs to encourage their participants to participate in exercises of value clarification where individuals are encouraged to reflect on what is important to them as a leader, to get in touch with their feelings. The source of authority for values is the individual self. Williams College professor James Nolan writes, "Where older moral orders looked to a transcendent being, to a covenantal community, to natural law, or to divine reason to provide the substantive basis for culture's moral boundaries, the therapeutic ethos establishes the self as the ultimate object of allegiance. . . . Where once the self was to be surrendered, denied, sacrificed, and died to, now the self is to be esteemed, actualized, affirmed, and unfettered."[3]

Almost all contemporary leadership discussions on character operate within core assumptions that are value-based and rooted in psychology—including positive psychology—rather than philosophy or religion. The goal of values-based leadership is authentic personal performance based on one's own personal truth. No matter what kind of words are used within this contemporary ethical frame to describe morals or values, this frame reverses, and eventually perverts traditional morality, traditional understandings of character, and traditional assumptions about the requirements of leadership. And when you drill down to the foundational level of leaders and teams, where relational competence is essential, you discover values based moral behavior renders both leaders and teams ineffective. The virtue proposition assumes a different frame.

Virtues appeal to an older philosophic and religious tradition in which morals are based in a transcendent objective reality. They exist outside of the self. They are part of the structure of reality. They are how the world works. They function like gravity, a universal objective reality that we deny at our own peril. They function like oxygen, a requisite for not just living a good life, but life itself. The virtue proposition acknowledges that there are objective moral criteria which, like gravity, like oxygen, impinge themselves on a person regardless of how he or she thinks or feels about them. They define the substance of character and are the standard by which the behavior of every leader is judged. When behavior—how one acts in a given circumstance—is aligned with virtues, we can speak of conduct: how one acts against transcendent moral criteria.

The goal of virtuous leadership is not personal authenticity but incremental alignment—alignment with reality, alignment to transcendent virtues. The goal of leadership development is not celebrating authentic performance but engaging in character formation, both the leader's and his or her team's. This involves habitually aligning one's conduct with virtue through the accountability of mentorship and lessons learned from experience. Virtues establish a vertical dimension to leadership governed by moral authority, in which morality is based in the structures of reality, not personal whim.

This virtues-based approach to the practical work of organizational and team leadership is essential for long-term success. Embracing it, acting within it, requires courage. The higher you go on the social and educational ladder, the greater the resistance there will be to the virtue proposition. I make no apology for such a contrarian approach because pragmatic success in actual organizational experience demands it. The virtue proposition accepts that there is no effective leadership without a prior commitment to objective morals, ultimate authority, or what we describe as transcendent virtues. The strongest case affirming the importance of the virtue proposition is the state of leadership among the world's contemporary leaders. It also stands atop millennia of ancient and current scholarship, globally shared religious tenets and practices, and the objective achievements by virtues-based leaders—from Buddha to Jesus, from Marcus Aurelius to Abraham Lincoln, from General Dwight Eisenhower to Dr. James Orbinsky (Doctors Without Borders)—across history.

I believe anyone who honestly reflects back on their life, on their participation with fellow students or colleagues, with teammates and within civic organizations, at your first or last job, among friends and family, will discover that more was accomplished—more good achieved—when character, virtues, and shared commitment to something greater than any individual guided their actions. This is a truism of my life.

Some learn it in a classroom or around a boardroom table. I learned it at the U.S. Naval Academy, on submarines, operating nuclear reactors, leading teams, serving as a parish pastor, succeeding and failing. I knew the people who met the challenges at Three Mile Island, Chernobyl, and Fukushima. Discussions of leadership in these settings are deadly serious. High performance teamwork is essential. There are no casual do-overs. Mistakes in these settings cost more than gold medals and quarterly revenue. Mistakes here can cost lives—something on the scope of Chernobyl. Conversely, leaders and teams animated by virtues-based decision and action will save lives. A commitment to the virtue proposition is why my path from nuclear engineer to pastor was short and straight.

This same level of concern followed me into retirement. I was haunted by the closing scene of *Schindler's List*. Oskar Schindler stands in the rail yard at his factory in Germany. His employees have gathered under the cover of darkness to say goodbye. In those final moments, he is given a letter signed by every employee thanking him for what he has done for them—saving them from the horrors of the Holocaust. Then he is presented with a gold ring inscribed in Hebrew with these words from the Talmud: "Whoever saves one life, saves the world entire."

The meaning is unmistakable: When a person shows humanity to another, he demonstrates the continuing existence of humanity in society. Schindler begins to weep and all he could say repeatedly is, "I could have gotten more out. I didn't do enough."[4] It is too easily forgotten that before Schindler became a revered secular saint, he was an industrialist, owner of a factory, a leader. His path from member of the Nazi Party and its military intelligence service to the man who wept because he didn't do enough to save the persecuted was not short or straight, but it was illuminated by virtues-based decisions and actions.

As I look back on my own life, the story of Oskar Schindler strikes a chord in me. I, too, could have done so much more. I cannot change the past, but I can work at shaping the future. I also know that if I am to make any kind of impact for the common good, I cannot do it alone. This was the genesis of the Severn Leadership Group.

The SLG is the crucible within which the insights, strategies, and practices explained in *The Virtue Proposition* were forged. Foundational to the Group is the belief that character matters to teams, and that teams are essential for effective organizations. The type of leadership that maximizes the effectiveness of teams is leadership of character based on transcendent virtues: the five virtues of love, integrity, truth, excellence, and relationships.

I believe a network of such teams will transform organizations—from small business to large complex companies—for the better. I believe that a network of such leaders across America will address the crisis of leadership we are experiencing. I also believe that such teams and leaders will foster superior organizational success through their honest alignment with human nature and reality. Finally, I believe that the measure of a leader is his ability to create a virtuous culture in which swing can be realized among their organizational team.

## Swing Is

When the three of us entered that smoke-filling compartment, visibility dropped, our breathing masks made communication difficult, and training took over. Training and something else, something more encompassing than training. I was the senior officer, but the other two knew more about the sequence of tasks that had to be completed to identify the cause of the fire and extinguish it. I became a leader in service to a team that had to perform at peak excellence. We were seamless, efficient, utterly focused, and successful. For the minutes we were isolated in that compartment, we experienced swing.

Virtuous leaders of virtuous teams seek the ineffable: in rowing it's called "swing," that moment when divergent strength achieves the synchronized harmony of high performance. This is that moment when, to quote Aristotle, "a kind of a whole is beyond its parts."[5] This is how an experienced oarsmen described swing:

Imagine that you are giving 110 percent effort to a task but because your fellow oarsmen are so much in synch that you can't feel any of their effort in any way that is different from yours. The result is feeling your own effort magnified by eight. The boat is moving powerfully but you can't differentiate between your effort and the effort of your teammates. The feeling is of power so much more than your own and it is amazing.[6]

Swing is the aspiration of all high performance teams—whether in a rowing shell, a submarine, a team, or an organization. This book is about developing leaders who create the conditions for swing. Swing is different from winning. Swing is the experience of pure teamwork realized while enduring the extremities of individual effort. Swing cannot be achieved by a lone rower in a single shell. That solitary rower might realize "flow," which is an individual experience. Swing is the result of totally aligned collective or team performance.

The skills needed to build a team are completely different from those which an already-functioning team calls on. Building that team first is a step that cannot be omitted, though we live and work in a world that routinely does. Over half of all workers are disengaged from their work. Large numbers engage in what has been called "quiet quitting." Not every collection of individuals, organization, or working group is a team. Teams require having shared performance results: a commitment to a compelling shared vision. But a shared vision is never enough. They must also have a mutual commitment to one another, most clearly evidenced through trust.

Jon Katzenbach and Douglas Smith describe a "team

performance curve" in their book, *The Wisdom of Teams: Creating the High-Performance Organization.* "Unlike teams," they explain, "working groups rely on the sum of 'individual bests' for their performance. They pursue no collective work product requiring joint effort." In contrast, a high performance team is evidenced by team members who are deeply committed to a common purpose as well as to one another. Katzenbach expands, "The best teams invest a tremendous amount of time and effort exploring, shaping, and agreeing on a purpose that belongs to them both collectively and individually."[7] The key to their success is a relational dynamic of mutuality, accountability, and trust. In rowing this creates the conditions for swing. It is the combination of a shared commitment to a compelling common cause coupled with the surrender of self to the benefit of other team members that creates high performance. Fostering leaders that create this environment is the aim of this book.

Rowing is the ultimate team sport. In a racing eight—a sixty-two-foot shell with eight oarsmen and one coxswain—eight powerfully fit individuals must harmonize the artistry of their stroke in a ballet of motion while individuals are experiencing their own individual hell. More than anything, rowing is mental resistance to pain while harmonizing one's performance to the others in the shell. The slightest deviation under race conditions can cause a disaster. There is no other sport that requires the sacrifice of self in service to the whole more than rowing. Legendary rowing coach and boat builder George Pocock said, "Rowing is perhaps the toughest of sports. Once the race starts, there are no time-outs, no substitutions. It calls upon the limits of human endurance. The coach must therefore impart the secrets of the special kind of endurance that comes from mind, heart, and body."[8] The sport demands the most of every individual. Author Daniel James Brown goes further, "No other sport demands and rewards the complete abandonment of the self the way that rowing does. . . . The team effort—the perfectly synchronized flow of muscle, oars, boat, and water; the single, whole, unified, and beautiful symphony that a crew in motion becomes—is all that matters. Not the individual, not the self."[9]

While demanding the most of every individual, rowing also demands the total synchronization of the individual effort to the other individuals at the point of greatest individual pain.

Swing only happens when all eight oarsmen are rowing in such perfect unison that no single action by any one rower is out of sync with those of the other. Only then will the boat continue to run out fluidly and gracefully between the pulls of the oars. Swing is the elusive overdrive of rowing. It is most often spoken of in spiritual terms. George Pocock asks, "Where is the spiritual value of rowing? The losing of self entirely to the cooperative effort of the crew as a whole."[10] The mystical, spiritual, and elusive ideal of swing *becomes* possible only when there is the kind of collaborative leadership that *makes* it possible.

Just reading this book will not produce such leaders. It is written to serve as an on-ramp for a personal and organizational journey in preparation, instruction, mentorship, and implementation. Starting it and completing it is up to you.

To begin, there are certain attitudes that one must adopt. There is no personal transformation in a leader without a high degree of self-awareness. One must acknowledge the need to start on such a journey. In addition, one must strive to embody certain behaviors. True leadership is not based on values but virtues. It is not about matters of your own choosing, which would be some form of values clarification, but rather aligning yourself to and embodying enduring transcendent virtues that are rooted in the structures of reality. A commitment to transcendent virtues is then filtered through a high level of emotional intelligence. Leadership is about being held accountable in practice to those virtues within the push and pull of everyday life. When a leader is capable of this, her conduct demonstrates her virtue intelligence, or VQ.

Clearly, there is no such thing as abstract accountability. The mark of a leader is only seen in application of character and skilled competence within an actual organization or a given team. It is not something that can be learned from a book or in a classroom. Its measure is actual lived reality with people under pressure. The combination of virtuous alignment, attitude, attributes, accountability, and application serve as the gristmill for the transformation of a difference-making leader. They change a leader's behavior and the culture of an organization.

Central in our journey together looms the figure of George Pocock. He is the legendary boat builder and rowing coach from the University of Washington. He serves as the philosophical Yoda of the rowing world. His insights on rowing serve as a direct metaphor on life. The story of nine Americans who won the gold medal at the 1936 Berlin Olympic games, a story told in Daniel James Brown's book, *The Boys in the Boat*, serves as this book's metaphorical backdrop. Pocock was a master team builder and the guru of swing. This concept serves as the master metaphor for this entire discussion about change-making leadership. Where this differs from other discussions of leadership is that, in this approach, the individual leader necessarily fades into the centrality of the team. This is a book about leaders who serve high performing teams, not a book about high performing leaders.

Leadership begins with you, but it is not about you.

My mission, and that of the SLG, is to foster virtues-driven leaders of character with a keen sense of emotional intelligence able to harness the personalities, abilities, and experiences of other people working in cohesive and synchronized teams to serve something larger than themselves. These are virtuous leaders able to exercise virtue intelligence as evidenced by their relational conduct within a team. This book explains how this can become a reality in your life and in your organization.

You are invited to participate in this aspirational movement of virtuous leadership. Let's begin the collective pilgrimage toward performance excellence, while making the world a better place, by becoming virtuous leaders creating virtuous organizations. This is the virtue proposition: leadership based on transcendent virtues filtered through emotional and virtue intelligence, coupled with technical competence, enabling organizations to achieve their greatest potential as high performance teams.

Let's begin.

# CHAPTER 1

---

# PRECONDITIONS OF PILGRIMAGE

*In a squad, you cannot have a crew without harmony. The men must like each other. There can't be any culls, there can't be any culls in the squad. The men have got to like each other. Eight hearts have to beat as one.*

— **GEORGE POCOCK**[1]

Leadership is frequently thought of as an arrival. "I have finally made it to the corner office!" This is a fallacy, most often held by new leaders. Leadership is not an arrival, but a departure. It is the invitation to begin an exploration or pilgrimage in learning about yourself and others.

Starting with the right attitude is key to becoming an effective leader. Cockiness is not a sign of leadership. Standing aloof, apart, and acting the hubristic know-it-all is the opposite of leadership. Too many leaders think that their power comes from knowing all the answers or giving the impression that they do. Nothing could be further from the truth.

If you enter a position of leadership with the confidence that you have all the answers, that you know how to turn this organization around, that you are the apex of wisdom, the smartest person in the room, your leadership will have failed even before you have started. The power of leadership isn't found in preening self-regard. It is found in character, vulnerability, humility, and the ability to return—not covet—authority. It is the opposite of an imperial leadership style. The adage about it being lonely at the top is a symptom of a brittle hierarchy rather than a collaborative, resilient leadership pattern. Author and entrepreneur Seth Godin expands on this when he warned,

> In an expert-run industrialized economy, there's a lot of pressure to be the one who's sure, the person with all the answers. Far more valuable is someone who has all the questions. The ability to figure out what hasn't been figured out and see what hasn't been seen is a significant advantage. Rarest of all is the person with the humility (and confidence) to realize that even the list of questions can remain elusive.[2]

Shared, collaborative authority and leadership encourages humility, encourages questioning. It is why effective organizations have a team at the top. In the Navy this is referred to as the command triad or the "big three"—the Commanding Officer, Executive Officer, and Command Master Chief. Unsurprisingly, the big three are almost uniformly comprised of deeply experienced officers.

Most complaints filed to the U.S. Equal Employment Opportunity Commission are against recently promoted leaders. The 2019 data shows that retaliation continues to be the most frequent charge filed with the agency, followed by disability, race, and sex. More interesting than the types of complaints waged are who they are primarily waged against. Most EEOC complaints are made against first-level managers shortly after they have been promoted to this new level of leadership. They are against new leaders, not old leaders.[3] Why might this be the case?

Newly made leaders confront opportunities and risks. Their roles bring responsibility and the opportunity for maturity and experience with essential technical competence. They also risk narrowing the scope of their courageous curiosity lest it be mistaken for their acknowledging how uncertain they might be in their new role. They would do better to mimic the habits of children, who almost always admit what they don't know precisely when they are first given greater responsibility.

In 1957, when I was in fifth grade, I was selected by my elementary school to become a Captain of School Safety Patrol and was invited to attend the Safety Patrol Summer Camp run by the Detroit Police Department. It was an honor I shared with boys from all around the city, one not diminished in the slightest by the fact that we were driven to the camp in blue Juvenile Correction Center buses. The manner of our arrival didn't lessen at all the understanding that we had arrived.

For a week our schedule started at 6:30 a.m., exercise at 7:00, breakfast at 7:30, and classes that went from 9:00 to 11:00. After that, it was lunch, games, sports, and swimming at a nearby lake. Except for those who couldn't swim, which included me. We were pulled aside for special instruction. A common feature throughout the camp was that from dining hall servers to camp counselors to classroom instructors, everyone was a police officer. And the swim instructors were former WWII Navy Frogman, the predecessors of today's Navy Seals. That each boy participating had been selected to become a "Captain" who would assume certain leadership positions of school safety when school started again never clouded our willingness to learn from Detroit's Finest. Each of us in that program brought courageous curiosity, expressed when we left home behind and climbed aboard those blue buses. We had no choice but to make new friends, forge relationships with our counselors, and learn new skills. It was maturity and competence that we brought back with us.

Too many adult leaders ignore that they are by definition beginning a pilgrimage. Often, they are encouraged to actively deny that fact. They are encouraged to assert that the new office, the new title, the higher salary all mark them as individuals who have arrived. In fact, they've only just begun a journey, one that if undertaken with courageous curiosity, character, and relational intelligence will help guarantee success.

Leadership at its best is embarking on a personal journey of exploration and discovery. The ancient Jewish poet captured this in the words of Psalm 84:5, "Blessed are those whose strength is in you, who have set their hearts on pilgrimage." If leadership is framed as a departure, it retains the fact that leadership is essentially an invitation for growth and learning. A willingness to change, a posture of self-reflectiveness, and openness to feedback are essential for effective leadership. This is the necessary starting attitude to someone becoming an effective leader. Ironically, it takes a strong leader—a leader with strong self-esteem—to know that he or she is not strong, does not have all the answers, and needs the help of others. Before a leader can be effective, a leader must have at their core this desire to grow, learn, and evolve as a person and as a person in relationship with others. Becoming a leader is about being open to critiquing and improving one's core character. Essential is a shift from closed to open, from having all the answers to having all the questions, from going it alone to going with others, from a static to a dynamic posture. Essential is sensing you are engaging in a lifetime of formation.

Stamped by my boyhood experiences in Detroit, as a teenager I declared my ambitions to be a naval officer, a pastor, or a state senator. My life journey led me to achieving two of those three. More important, however, is the connective thread across all of those early ambitions: a call to make a difference, to serve others, and to work with others to bring about good. That thread runs through my careers as an officer, a nuclear engineer, an executive and international director, and as a local pastor. The work of making a difference is a journey of ability, courage, and optimism. It begins with you.

The call to leadership is the invitation to embark on a pilgrimage whereby you commit to becoming the best possible version of yourself. Leadership is about change. Change that begins with you, transforms you, and permeates all with whom you come into contact. The first step in effective leadership is the willingness to be self-reflective, self-critical:

Who am I?
What am I about?
Why do I behave as I do?
What virtues align my life?

These are not easy questions. They are questions people tend to avoid, and they are questions that busyness tends to push to the backburner. The mistake isn't in not having answers, however. The mistake is in not facing the difficult questions. Leadership is not about having it all figured out by yourself, but knowing that you need the help of others to become the best version of yourself.

The first irony of leadership is that the way up is down.

You must look inward, with the help of others. There are no elite athletes who think that they can become the best version of themselves without a coach. Having a mentor, a coach, an advisor is not a sign of weakness but a foundational sign that you are ready for leadership, that you have adopted a posture of learning and growth. This is essential for you to become a person worthy of leadership. This is the internal gaze framed by the first question of personhood: "Who am I?"

The second irony of leadership is that it's not about the leader.

It is essential that you have the right external gaze. In business, leadership generally involves assuming the responsibility for a team, a division, an organization. Leadership is thus often framed as furthering the organization's ambitions, whether measured in expanding its influence or increasing its revenue. To do this successfully requires an answer to the foundational question, "What is my purpose?" What we decide is the ultimate purpose of our lives, and what virtues define it, will frame our leadership decisions and our allocation of time, money, and effort. Knowing who you are, and what your purpose is, permits effective leadership.

Harvard Business School professor Clayton Christensen

writes, "It is one thing to see into the foggy future with acuity and chart the course corrections that the company must make. But it's quite another to persuade employees who might not see the changes ahead to line up and work cooperatively to take the company in that new direction."[4] The purpose of a leader is not identifying organizational goals, but animating performance in others, namely building up people. Put simply, the measure of a leader is their ability to build a team.

The two ironies of leadership are mutually reinforcing. When leaders are humble enough to know that they do not have all the answers and thereby adopt a collaborative leadership style, it makes it easier for them to allocate their resources around building a team. Leadership becomes more about listening than telling, more about people than spreadsheets.

In our values-based world, listening and attending to people go unmeasured.

There are lots of problems with quarterly or annual performance reviews as they are typically conducted. Typically, the criteria being used for evaluations are framed by technical competence and benchmark achievements. What if this were completely changed? What if, rather than only measuring technical competence, a leader's performance was first judged on his ability to build the conditions for a cohesive high performance team?

If we put first things first, building up people and the cohesion of the team—the degree of swing—then secondary things like ability to generate sales, customer satisfaction, technical competence, and shareholder value will take care of themselves. However, relational strengths are not what is typically measured in a leader's performance review.

In rowing, when we focus on the athletes' two-kilometer erg times, or the time of the shell under race conditions against other competitors—as important as these measures may be—we have failed to focus on the internal spiritual factor that makes all the difference in the boat's performance: the relational dynamics between the oarsmen themselves, their sense of being a team. Do they like each other? Are eight hearts beating as one?

Too often we know the absence of swing before we experience it. When I entered the U.S. Naval Academy in 1964, I had never seen an ocean and was more familiar with the miniature ships plying the model-yacht basin at Belle Isle on the Detroit River than the inside of a warship. I was also no athlete. Urban Detroit allowed for a little baseball, but that was about it. So, I opted to row plebe summer and first year. It demanded long runs, extensive conditioning, hours and hours of rowing on the Severn River in rain, snow, and ice. Months and months of training to compete in two thousand-meter, eight-man shell races lasting less than eight minutes.

We never came close to swing. Individually, we all got into great physical shape. Individually, we all strove to optimize our strokes. We never fell into sustained synch. During one race I watched as a teammate failed to pick up the pace on the order to and caught a "crab" (his oar momentarily caught in the water) and flipped out of the boat. He was not hurt, nor was the boat, but we never finished the race.

The true test of leadership is the leader's ability to create internal alignment among the members of her team. This is the invisible culture that lifts the abilities of individuals to a sum that is greater than the parts. The measure of a leader is his ability to create the conditions for a cohesive team with swing. A leader cannot create swing, only the conditions for swing. Swing is created only by the team, eight rowers and a coxswain, but never without the input from the coach. Leadership is a relational art as much as a technical science.

Rowing is a very technical sport that easily attracts type A technical engineers. Consequently, there is math and statistics about every aspect of rowing. But there is more to rowing than its technical dimensions. Understanding this was the genius of George Pocock who, as a wooden boatbuilder, combined marine engineering with the art of a craftsman and the empathy of a counselor. The task of building a fragile and delicately tuned racing shell has been aptly likened to the making of a fine violin. In fact, one of Pocock's boatbuilding team, Hilmer Lee, was a violin maker in his spare time. Pocock focused on the hearts and souls of his young oarsmen. He worked toward achieving this mystical, spiritual–emotional alignment between highly competitive individual men, each fighting each other for a seat in the boat.

Because Pocock was able to consistently create such alignment in racing shells, he became the "high priest" of the University of Washington rowing program. Years later, Washington oarsmen would remember that when they stood in his presence, responded to his leadership, they were in the presence of a leader who had come to symbolize this ineffable sacred thing. The goal of achieving swing was always before them. It is my goal for you to become just such a leader.

For such a leader, a combination of transcendent virtues and emotional intelligence are basic requirements. While this swing in a rowing shell is a rare thing, it is not impossible to achieve when a team combines with a certain kind of leader. Such leaders can be developed. Such teams can be realized. Swing is possible. Required is a systems-based leadership approach that is grounded in three basic assumptions:

First, leadership is defined by your character.

Second, character is shaped by timeless transcendent virtues.

Third, selfless courage and servant leadership are learned behaviors that reflect moral conduct.

Having the right attitude is essential. Knowing the questions you need answers to is essential. You must frame leadership as a departure, an adventure in change and learning, and you must recognize that leadership is not about the leader but the team. These are the prerequisites for pilgrimage. Leadership can be learned. This is where the learning begins.

# CHAPTER 2

---

# FACING IN THE
# RIGHT DIRECTION

*The opposite of rowing is drifting.*
— GEORGE POCOCK[1]

In 1979 I was a third-year seminary student. During an internship at a church just outside of Columbus, Ohio, I was directed by two superb supervisors, the pastor at the church, Dr. Dave Shugert, and my seminary advisor, the Professor of Pastoral Care, Dr. Art Becker.

Toward the end of that internship, I had a meeting with Dr. Becker. I shared some of my experiences, he offered me insight and guidance. As we talked about a difficult case involving a parishioner confronting a tragedy, Dr. Becker asked me a question that stopped me dead in my tracks.

"What were you feeling, Sig?"

My years in seminary hadn't changed the fact that I was a trained nuclear engineer. Around reactors being able to gather, assess, and lay out all relevant facts and issues had been the uppermost importance. How I felt about any of them was irrelevant. Wasn't it?

Dr. Becker brought home to me the truth that to be an effective leader, as engineer or pastor, I needed facts *and* feelings. My success on submarines and around nuclear reactors hadn't been due to an absence of emotion, but its implicit presence, for my fellow submariners, for my fellow engineers, for all the lives our skilled work intersected with.

Trained, experienced competence is absolutely necessary. Clarity of goals—whether they arise within a company or within a church, is absolutely necessary. Exceeding those goals requires something more: relational competence, which begins with the relationship you have with yourself.

The direct line from a team that exceeds its performance goals and their leader is found in the character of that leader.

Since leadership is not an arrival, but a departure, you need to know where you are planning to go. For the virtuous leader—the leader who grasps that *why* matters as much, or even more than *how*—they must know themselves. An effective leader needs to reflect early on how he or she will measure their life. What is a good life? How will I get there? Leadership demands having a clear destination and an internal moral compass to guide your decisions to get you there.

Too often we do not have a meaningful strategy for our lives. We might map out a career strategy for how to get ahead within a particular organization. But this is not a leadership strategy any more than it is a life strategy. It's running a race with blinders on. We may go fast but we will be off course. An effective leader must choose the right direction and be grounded in that direction with the right disciplines to get there. Hindsight is too late.

Swimming is a mandatory skill for midshipmen at the U.S. Naval Academy. With few exceptions, swimming wasn't something I did much growing up in Detroit. Now came my first test at the Academy. After swimming for what seemed like an eternity, I heard yelling, "Berg, Berg come back, come back!" I had gotten halfway across the pool and then somehow, I had taken a slow turn to port and headed out to sea.

When I returned, the instructor was waiting for me. "Your stroke looked pretty good, but where were you going? Were you swimming with your eyes closed?"

I nodded. All the reprimand I got was a sad shaking of the instructor's head. It was also all I needed.

This experience taught me two valuable lessons. First, keep your eyes open and focus on the mark. If you don't, you will lose your way. Second, it is important to have people willing to call you back when you are off course.

What is apparent to all older leaders is that you cannot achieve excellence by accident. You must keep your eyes open, listen to others, and especially attend to your own character. Effective leadership takes consciously determined self-reflection.

From a self-taught habit of self-reflection, you can make considered, and better, decisions. Over the course of a life, it is the accumulation of small decisions that shape who you are, the life you have. Most lives do not consist of sharp turns and about-faces. Rather, they consist of undetected drift, the accumulation of a thousand little unconsidered decisions. Author Annie Dillard writes, "How we spend our days is, of course, how we spend our lives."[2] Her point? If you want to know what you will be like in twenty years, take a good look at the small decisions you are making today. Your life is the sum of your days. Tomorrow never comes.

The same holds for the achievements of any team, any organization. So, too, a race is the accumulation of a thousand separate strokes.

Rowing is one of the few sports where one looks backward to go forward. This is the way pre-industrial English river men rowed their boats. Boats are rowed backward because the muscle power in rowing comes from the big muscles in the legs, back, and shoulders. Steering the shell efficiently while looking backward is difficult, especially in head races with staggered starts rowed on a winding river. During these races, crashes of oars and boats are not uncommon. Because a narrow sixty-two-foot shell is hard to steer, it is imperative to set your sights in the right direction early in the process. Last-minute changes in direction are rarely effective.

The same can be said about effective leadership.

Teams and organizations realize results on the basis of the core convictions that animate them. What is true for teams is no less true for individuals. Just as your individual core convictions are not shaped by conscious life-and-death decisions but by the small, seemingly inconsequential unconscious decisions you make every day, so are the convictions that animate and direct teams. Commitment to convictions is the covenant—implicit or explicit—that runs between teams and individuals, followers and leaders. When our lives become a series of extenuating circumstances, an ongoing series of cheat days, we eventually realize that our core principles have been abandoned for something else. We are drifting.

All effective leaders must answer these questions:

1.  What is the good life? More specifically, what are the metrics of success for your life?
2.  How does one achieve the good life? More specifically, do you have an inner compass that will guide your daily choices?

When viewed from the vantage point of age and history, every leader's life is an eventual, inevitable answer to these questions. It is not *whether* you will give an answer with your life, only will you be *conscious* of the choices you are making in time for those choices to make a difference?

So ask yourself, are you rowing or drifting?

Immediately a second question arises. How would you know?

*New York Times* columnist David Brooks speaks of the difference between résumé virtues and eulogy virtues, "The résumé virtues are the skills you bring to the marketplace. The eulogy virtues are the ones that are talked about at your funeral— whether you were kind, brave, honest, or faithful. Were you capable of deep love?"[3] We instinctively know that the eulogy virtues are more important, but then everything in our professional and cultural life biases the other. We may believe that people matter most, but most of the incremental choices we make in life say otherwise.

These eulogy virtues are closely tied to our moral core or character. They serve as a compass to guide the leader in their relational dynamics and organizational decisions over time. Leadership development is a lifelong experience. It is incrementally transformational.

As the leader of a team, the extent to which you and your

team are drifting or rowing is visible in the team's relational dynamic, which is determined by its leader.

It is often at this point when introducing the virtue proposition of leadership that someone will express doubts; Yes, character matters, and a good character matters for living a good life, the doubter will allow. And an inner compass is valuable for everyone. But does this really apply to a team leader working to help an organization realize profits, increase market share, and improved product development?

Yes, absolutely. Because we must accomplish and live within relationships, character matters profoundly, always.

In 2002, I was the Managing Director of the World Association of Nuclear Operators (WANO), located in London. WANO exists to unite "every company and country in the world that has an operating commercial nuclear power plant to achieve the highest possible standards of nuclear safety."[4] That is a performance goal no sane person could argue with. However, how to achieve this performance goal, especially among nations with different languages, cultures, and even possibly histories of adversarial relationships, was the stuff of arguments. During what was a frustrating two-year tenure as WANO's managing director, I had accomplishments and setbacks. One exchange, however, convinced me that what was achieved boiled down to trust in my team's and my character.

A senior leader of a foreign delegation once told me, "We are different than you Americans." He paused, then continued, "My people have been watching you and they all tell me the same thing, 'You can trust him. He is honest.'" He then looked me in the eye. "Most importantly, you respect us." Our friendship declared, our teams had dinner and progress was made.

This book embraces the template visible in the great examples of leaders who lived lives following the "golden rule," which calls leaders to love one another, serve others, and seek the common good. Harvard Business School professor Clayton Christensen warns, "MBA students come to school thinking that a career in business means buying, selling, and investing in companies. That's unfortunate. Doing deals doesn't yield the deep rewards that come from building up people."[5] The good life for an effective leader is not measured in dollars invested, but in individuals whose lives you've touched. For leaders of teams, this relational dynamic is immediate and unavoidable.

The heart of leadership is the revealed character of the leader, character shaped by virtues and beliefs imbedded in one's inner being. They serve as one's inner compass and in the end, they direct actions, shape conduct, and shape your sphere of influence. The character of the leader determines the destination he or she will achieve. They are the leader's essential core. I believe that leadership is not defined by a particular style, skill set, or desired outcome. Rather, leadership is defined by one's moral core.

As human beings, each of us has a moral core. It is called our character. If that core is not protected, bad things will happen. When the winds of darkness blow, the heat of conflict sears, and every ounce of our strength is drained, how do we react? Do we under conditions of pressure and testing remain true to our core and the virtues that define it? Our core serves as our moral compass that guides us on the decisions we make on the journey to our destination.

## Transcendent Virtues

Our moral core is our character, which is revealed in our conduct. As we have seen, a stable character is based on transcendent virtues. Values will not suffice. If your life is held accountable to moral values you will drift, for, as we have seen, values are like your choice of ice cream flavor. Virtues are like submitting to gravity. Virtues are not optional or driven by opinion. Historic transcendent virtues are common to all cultures and are derived from multiple sources. C.S. Lewis referred to them as the "Tao."[6]

A commonly recognized and full-flowering example of virtues is seen in the historic life of Jesus of Nazareth. For effective team-oriented leadership, there are five virtues that are essential for the creation of high performancee teams: Love, Integrity, Truth, Excellence, and Relationships. We will explore these virtues in more depth in the next chapter. Here I'll discuss further how virtues function in general in our lives.

Virtues are not revealed in abstractions, but in daily living. They are the guiding framework for the many small decisions we make each day. They are what keep us on track, stroke by stroke, as we head down the racecourse. Virtues are not something you make up or choose, rather they are something to which you submit and align yourself to throughout the race. While they are largely invisible, as a person's character is not immediately seen, they are always revealed in your behavior and its alignment to your code of conduct. Every life is guided by this hidden core. Your character is revealed in your conduct, particularly under pressure.

The question then is whether your character is fully aligned or in the process of being aligned to those transcendent virtues that define effective leadership. It is not enough to know these virtues, being able to quickly rattle off the list of five virtues—love, integrity, truth, excellence, and relationships. What is necessary is to unconsciously embody these virtues through repeated practice, habituation, and accountability. Neuroscience informs us that only about 5 percent of our choices are under our direct rational control at any one time. Most of our behaviors are shaped by our unconscious habituated beliefs and virtues.[7] Consequently, three steps are involved in virtue formation.

First, we must know what these virtues entail and have our imaginations shaped by the lives of notable exemplars of these virtues. Second, we must practice these virtues during daily life. They are not learned from a book but embodied through daily living. And finally, as we are all inclined to rationalize our behavior and fail to see ourselves and our behaviors clearly, we need others to hold us accountable to the high standards that these transcendent virtues demand in daily life. We need others to confirm our behavior aligns with our code of conduct. All serious athletes need a coach to perform at their best, so, too, all serious leaders need a mentor who is personally aligned to these transcendent virtues to call them to the best version of themselves in practice. Serious formation in virtues requires a mentor.

To prepare to be an effective leader, we must have a teachable spirit and a willingness to change. We must recognize that the true destination of leadership is the empowering of others, the building of teams. To arrive at that destination, our daily decisions need to be shaped by transcendent core virtues. As these decisions are largely unconscious, we must seek to embody and habituate these virtues.

Swing in a team involves more than the harmony of external technique. It also involves the harmony of internal alignment to these invisible transcendent virtues. It is not in the plan prior to the race where the race is won, but in the consistent performance of every stroke during the race. Rowers may be facing backward, but when their destination is clear and their daily decisions aligned to a shared transcendent core, the shell moves forward with a strength of purpose and in an unwavering direction. These are the crews that exceed their individual capabilities and potential. These are the crews that, rather than drift, achieve swing.

# CHAPTER 3

---

# THE INVISIBLE CORE

*Building a boat was like religion. It wasn't enough to master the technical details of it. You had to give yourself up to it spiritually; you had to surrender yourself absolutely to it. When you were done and walked away from the boat, you had to feel that you had left a piece of yourself behind in it forever, a bit of your heart.*

— GEORGE POCOCK[1]

Buried in every leader is an inner, invisible core. It is from this core that the character and effectiveness of the leader emerges. It may be mysterious, but it is the source of their mastery. Unpacking that mystery begins with a focus on the visible consequences of a leader's conduct.

Over the years, I have served as a chief engineer on a nuclear submarine and later as the site vice president of a commercial nuclear power complex with two 1250-megawatt pressurized water reactors (PWR). As one who had overall responsibility for reactor operations, I also had the additional duty of being the reactor's conscience. I was to ensure that each reactor was properly operated, maintained, and that the people with whom I worked were well trained. My job was to protect the reactor core. If I did not, bad things would happen.

There is more to bad things not happening than what can be seen. Visible is a properly operating reactor. Invisible is the collective conscience of my team in making sure it did.

Similarly, there is more to a rower than can be seen. This was the mystery of Joe Rantz, the great rower on the 1936 Olympic team. University of Washington rowing varsity coach Al Ulbrickson and freshman coach Tom Bolles recognized that they had a problem with Rantz.

> Ulbrickson had been studying Joe for a year now, ever since Tom Bolles had first warned him that the boy was touchy and uneven, that there were days when he could row like quicksilver—so smooth and fluid and powerful that he seemed a part of the boat and his oar and the water all at once—and days when he was downright lousy. Since then, Ulbrickson had tried everything—he'd scolded Joe, he'd encouraged him, he'd demoted him, he'd repromoted him. But he wasn't any closer to understanding the mystery of him. Now Ulbrickson turned to Pocock for help.[2]

Pocock invited the boy into his workshop where he was building wooden shells. He talked about the tools and the different characteristics of the wood used in the building of shells. "The wood, Pocock murmured, taught us about survival, about overcoming difficulty, about prevailing over adversity, but it also taught us something about the underlying reason for surviving in the first place. Something about infinite beauty, about undying grace, about things larger and greater than ourselves. 'Sure, I can make a boat,' he said, and then added, 'but only God can make a tree.'"

The building of the shell and the character of the wood became a metaphor for Joe's life. It was a strategic indirection that broke through Joe's defensive barriers that hid his internal turmoil and woundedness reflected in his deep insecurity, lack of acceptance, and inability to trust. Pocock concluded, "Rowing is like building a wooden shell. And a lot of life is like that too, the parts that really matter anyway. Do you know what I mean, Joe?"[3]

Pocock was able to touch Rantz's mysterious inner rower. The moral core of the rower is the heartbeat of the crew. Ulbrickson was wise in taking the invisible core of Rantz seriously. He was wise to put his psychological guru, George Pocock, on to the task. Until Rantz could overcome his inability to trust his fellow oarsmen in the boat, swing would remain elusive. Often overlooked by leaders, the invisible core of the team member ultimately makes the difference between average and superior performance in a team. You must attend to the moral core of your team and then protect it vigilantly.

A leader's character is the leader's core. Because the leader's core is the axis of the relational dynamic between leader and team, it must be developed, nurtured, and protected at all costs. One is not able to lead others well without the virtues of love, integrity, truth, excellence, and healthy relationships. The same is true for every team member. These are the prerequisites for every leader and follower.

They are:

## Love

- Serves others before self
- Seeks to inspire others
- Aims to build the capacity of others
- Believes in his team
- Displays empathy and compassion
- Treats others with respect
- Does not humiliate another person, group, or adversary
- Listens, asks questions
- Cares for her own personal well-being
- Willing to say, "No!"
- Can be tough or challenging when necessary

## Integrity

- Says what is important and acts accordingly
- Aligns personal, family, and professional lives
- Doing the right thing when no one is watching
- Self-aware, self-controlled, outward-focused
- Willing to admit being wrong
- Appreciates personal feedback
- Pursues consistent conduct
- Remains humble

## Truth

- Able to distinguish between what is right and what is wrong
- Recognizes the difference between fact and opinion
- Aware of who "I am" and who "I am not."

- Realistic about self, circumstances, conditions
- Willing to stand up for what is right
- Willing to speak up when something is wrong
- Is honest

## Excellence

- Strives daily to learn, grow, and improve
- Seeks conduct consistent with a life of character and integrity
- Builds the capacity and skills of others
- Brings the best out in people
- Sets high standards
- Holds people accountable
- Develops a positive and engaging work environment

## Relationships

- Recognizes leadership is about people, not things
- Knows and cares about his or her people
- Listens, encourages, teaches
- Provides constructive feedback
- Focuses on people, not career
- Seeks the common good
- Builds trust
- Remains approachable

These virtues do not, and cannot, work in isolation; they must be integrated, they must work together. Consider the example of courage. It is the virtue of courage that integrates all these other virtues together at their point of greatest testing. It takes courage to be a leader and follower. It takes courage to love others before the self. It takes courage to be a difference-maker.

Another way that these disparate virtues are integrated is around the concept of flourishing. Flourishing, within yourself, a team, an organization, paves the way to the authenticity that comes from the ability, as described by Andy Crouch, to "be both strong and weak" at the same time.[4] Flourishing forces us to face who we are. It requires us to embrace both our strengths and weaknesses, our dreams and fears, and even life and death. Flourishing—which has also been termed enlightenment, transcendence, and tranquility in other practices and faiths—allows us to pursue greater authority and greater vulnerability at the same time. Flourishing occurs when rising "authority and vulnerability" are held in tension. Only when we embrace being both "strong and weak" can our true character emerge, enabling us to become the best version of ourselves.

Leadership starts with us, but it ends with others. If we are driven with a sense of who we are and what we are about, then there is a wholeness that gives us the courage to be a leader and a follower, confident and humble, demanding and empathetic, able to listen and able to give commands. An effective leader has drive without being driven. Becoming a leader is a process, but it begins with being a follower.

The process of leadership development starts with the doable, for everyone is capable of being a follower. It begins with the ability to take an honest look at yourself, to acknowledge your own shortcomings and areas needing improvement. Leadership demands embracing the process of transformation. We might start with asking,

- Who am I?
- What is my purpose?
- What are my strengths and weaknesses?
- Where am I today and what are my dreams for tomorrow?
- Is there a better version of myself?
- Am I willing to change?

Change can be tracked by using an Individual Change Model.

## Individual Change Model

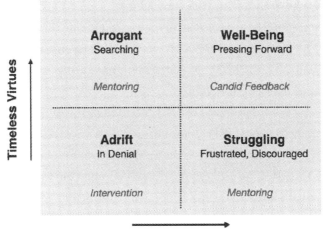

There are two variables that are essential in this change model: the degree of self-reflection and the degree of alignment to the transcendent virtues. This sets up a four-quadrant change model:

1. **Adrift:** low self-reflection/low virtue recognition.
2. **Struggling:** high self-reflection/low virtue recognition.
3. **Arrogant:** low self-reflection/high virtue recognition; and
4. **Well-being:** high self-reflection/high virtue recognition.

The person who is adrift is not open to change and the timeless virtues play no role in his life. His core is not well-developed. Adrift and in denial, he does not know why, how, or what to change. Needed here is an outside intervention to break through the paralysis of inaction.

A person who is struggling wants to change but doesn't know where to begin. He is struggling, often frustrated, and discouraged. He knows why he needs to change but does not know how or which behaviors to change. The most effective intervention would be an outside mentor coupled with an abundance of encouragement.

A person who is arrogant recognizes the importance of the LITER virtues but lacks personal self-awareness. Her aspirations do not match her conduct. She knows how to behave, but without self-awareness she doesn't adopt behaviors aligned with what she knows. She is deceived about herself and the people she serves. This person can assume a kind of arrogant hypocritical self-deception that borders on arrogance. Here, too, a mentor is critical.

A person enjoys well-being when he both desires change and is seeking to integrate the timeless virtues into his life. He knows both what needs to be done and, as he does what is needed, he experiences a degree of authenticity and purpose in his life. It is not that this person is perfect, but he is self-aware and purposeful in the process of becoming the best version of himself, with the aim of helping others.

Leadership begins by embracing this transformative process toward becoming your most authentic self in service to others. Here the leader is freed to flourish and knows that she has made a real difference in the lives of others. To this end, the leader protects the core, her own and the team's.

There are certain attitudes that serve as preparation for effective leadership. In this introductory section we have examined four of them:

1. A leader must be teachable, open to learn, and willing to change. Leadership is the beginning of a journey of growth.

2. A leader must realize that leadership is mainly about people: serving, empowering, and encouraging them. This is especially so when leadership is measured by its ability to create an effective team.

3. To maintain a consistent people-oriented focus, a leader's incremental daily decisions need to be grounded in a steady commitment to certain transcendent virtues: love, integrity, truth, excellence, and relationships. Every effective team needs to be aligned together to these transcendent virtues.

4. Finally, leaders reveal their commitment in the daily practice of leadership. What you say and think is important, but it is only your conduct that matters. It is only your consistent conduct that reveals your true core commitments. To stay on track, all leaders need an outside mentor or truth-teller to hold him accountable.

All leaders must consciously lean against groupthink in favor of celebrating contrarian input.[5] At King Arthur's Roundtable, this was a function served by Merlin, the wise sage, and Dragonet, the court jester.

These are the attitudes that are needed as you embark on a journey of growth: humility, people-orientation, virtues, and accountability. A leader needs a desire to grow, a virtues-established direction, and an unwavering destination in his sights to be achieved with others. These are the attitudes that an effective leader must embody. Attitudes are internal to the leader. Self-evidently, however, no leader completes the journey alone. Within an organization, within a team, the leader acts within relationships among colleagues, team members, followers. Correct attitudes in the leader fuel effective leadership attributes in the organization. Attributes, to which we now turn, are the objective characteristics of the leadership dynamic itself.

# CHAPTER 4

*DIFFERENCE-MAKER DYNAMIC*

*From the moment the shell is launched, the coxswain is the captain of the boat. He or she must exert control, both physically and psychologically, over everything that goes on in the shell. Good coxes know their oarsmen inside and out—their individual strengths and vulnerabilities—and they know how to get the most out of each man at any given moment. They have the force of character to inspire exhausted rowers to dig deeper and try harder, even when all seems lost. . . . In short, a good coxswain is a quarterback, a cheerleader, and a coach all in one. He or she is a deep thinker, canny like a fox, inspirational, and in many cases the toughest person in the boat.*

— **DANIEL JAMES BROWN**[1]

The relationship between leaders and followers is often overlooked. But when it is witnessed, when its relational strength is visible in games won, achievements realized, against-the-odds accomplishments, from boardroom to battlefield, obtaining it can seem mystical. We invoke the historical examples with reverence: the 1969 Mets, General Motors in the late 2000s, the 111-win streak of the UConn Women's Basketball team, the Battle of the Bulge. To make the mystical relatable, we reduce it to an individual: Mets' pitcher Tom Seaver, or Anthony Clement McAuliffe, acting commander of the 101st Airborne Division during the WWII Battle of the Bulge. When discussions of leadership see only the mystical or the exceptional individual, they miss the essential contribution of followership. In every instance, however, it is in the relationship of leader to follower where the difference-maker dynamic is found.

Leadership is not a linear process that can be taken apart. It is not a noun but a verb. It is an ongoing synergistic dynamic that can only be looked at correctly as a whole. Because its axis is an inner core comprised of bedrock virtues, what many perceive as being mysterious is in fact closer to being something spiritual that can be understood in secular terms. It is a common commitment to outcomes pursued while following virtues reflected in character and visible in conduct.

We have looked at this difference-making relationship from the perspective of the attitudes of the individual leader. We now look at the same relationship from the perspective of the attitudes that characterize an organization where effective leadership is present. It is confirmed by evidence of swing. Swing is the practice consequence of competent leaders and followers with a common commitment acting by this mystical, holistic, spiritual concept.

It is the leader's responsibility to create the conditions of swing. Amid these conditions, the team members themselves achieve swing. To put this in its sharpest focus, consider the relationship between the coxswain and the stroke. The coxswain gives the commands, establishes the stroke rate, but it is the stroke who translates the coxswain's words into action within the shell. To narrow this relationship to their functional roles is to miss the hidden dynamic that makes the difference. Most teams, most leaders, however, do precisely this. Jobs are to be done. Assignments are to be completed. Typically, the attitude is that leaders think and the hired hands do the work. This traditional model extends a fig leaf of hope to the workers. Someday the follower can escape from the gulag and become a leader himself. This perspective encourages the current gulf that exists between far too many leaders and their followers. This perspective does not create a high level of employee engagement or trust, leading to disillusionment and poor retention—resulting in mediocre performance.

This is not an attitude that will foster high performance teams or swing. In most organizations, however, it is the expected norm and the dysfunctional status quo. To attain the former, and bring an end to the latter, the relationship between the leader and the follower must be further explored.

The leader and the follower share a core commitment that galvanizes their identity, character, and conduct. They share a common mission, intent, or goal—why the group exists. Both the follower and the leader pursue the purpose with dedication and passion. Note, however, that at this level the dynamic is external and abstract whether winning a championship or exceeding quarterly sales goals.

For exceptional results to be achieved, however, it depends on the relational dynamic between the leader and the follower.

The dynamic must shift from the abstract to the personal.

The essential role of a leader is to inspire his followers. When that occurs, you can expect followers to develop higher levels of trust. With trust arises a shared dedication to integrity, and with shared integrity a relational form of love. Together love, integrity, and truth allow for excellent relationships conducive of swing. The leader feels supported, so, too, do her followers, and the organization sees improved levels of performance. The cycle then repeats itself. Over time, the process is reinforced, and it becomes self-sustaining. This mutually reinforcing relational dynamic based on mutual respect and affection serves as the flywheel within a high performance team. Conversely, an adversarial relationship at this organizational junction is a recipe for disaster.

The relationship dynamic inherent to difference-making allows us to define followership and leadership as:

Followership is a relationship of purpose. The follower is a member of the team or organization focused on and committed to a common purpose. Each person has a role to play if the purpose is to be accomplished. The follower is inspired and energized to fulfill that role, knowing that any weak link in the chain could well lead to failure. He supports the leader by communicating what is working and what is not. A resulting atmosphere prevails that breeds honesty, commitment, and trust throughout the organization. At its best, it is a relationship of mutual affection. The follower is a key difference-maker.

Leadership is a relationship of influence. It is not a positional description. A person with a position of responsibility may not be a leader. Likewise, a leader may not always have a job title or described position. Leadership is a variable of relational influence. The leader's distinct role is to see beyond the horizon, to challenge and shape outcomes while encouraging, teaching, and caring for those in her charge. They are good listeners. They seek constructive feedback. Leaders develop teams, not careers. Leaders serve their followers. Leaders create the conditions for swing. The leader is a key difference-maker.

But what makes the difference between a team capable of swing and one not capable is the conscious awareness that follower and leader are inseparably interconnected. Leadership and followership are all about people and relationships. It is personal and collaborative. When successful, there is an attachment based on love. There is an awareness that one cannot succeed without one another. This reverses and transforms the typical modern hierarchical management dynamics. Positional authority of the leader becomes team authority of mutuality.

This kind of leader is not born but can be developed over time. Individuals aspiring to lead need time to create a sense of purpose, self-awareness, mutual understanding, a sense of humility, and embody the virtues in practice. The difference-making dynamic is a mutual attachment between leaders and followers based on respect and love.

At the heart of this process is the development of core virtues. The virtues serve as a compass to guide the team members through life, particularly in those critical moments when a focused mind and thoughtful decisions are needed. Particularly in those critical moments when courage is required. One must do more than just think about these virtues, one must come to think with these virtues. It is in the dynamic of mutually thinking with the team in a shared life under pressure that respect, mutuality, and affection emerge into the difference-maker dynamic.

All leadership development begins by being a good follower—because being a good leader means sacrificing for the team. Followership provides the opportunity for core virtues to be shaped, technical ability to become competent, solid work habits and standards to develop, the ability to give and receive feedback to be fostered, and teamwork to be experienced. The foundational competencies necessary for a follower are the fundamental attributes required of a leader.

Leaders capable of demonstrating humility to their team play a critical role in developing followers. A leader's behavior is always in full view. Followers quickly learn if a leader is engaged or distant, practices what she preaches, sets high standards and holds people accountable, listens and shows empathy for others, receives, and provides constructive feedback, and is self-serving or not. The conduct of a leader influences the practices of the follower. The imprint can be lifelong. It is also through virtuous behavior that a leader builds the capacity of her followers. This entails teaching, encouraging, and developing the skills and abilities of each person on the team. It's all about helping followers succeed now *and* in the future. In this environment, people feel valued and supported. It leads to an engaged workforce as it is based on mutual attachment.

Leaders and followers do not work in isolation. They are an interconnected system that is pivotal for team success.

After my first tour at sea on a nuclear submarine, the Navy sent me to its prototype reactor facility near Idaho Falls, Idaho. It was here that the Navy trained and certified both officers and enlisted to operate a Navy nuclear power plant. I was to lead a crew of officers and enlisted tasked with training other officers and enlisted in the S1W prototype reactor, the same reactor used on the USS *Nautilus*, the first nuclear submarine.

On arrival I was informed that I would be the Leading Engineering Officer of the Watch on Crew A. Shortly after arrival, I was informed that Crew A had the lowest performance record for getting its students qualified and qualified on time.

The reactor facility operated twenty-four hours a day, seven days a week. There were four training crews, A through D. The work cycle was for three crews to train on eight-hour rotating shifts, with the fourth crew off work for five days. Each student was expected to study an additional four hours on site, either before or after his normal eight-hour shift. This regimen lasted six months for each cohort of students, both enlisted and officer. This was the context within which Crew A would have to improve.

A crew was made up of a Submarine Officer, Reactor Operators, Electricians, and Machinist Mates, all pulled from sea assignments to be instructors. Each crew had a highly experienced Chief Petty Officer, a qualified civilian instructor from Bettis Atomic Power Laboratories, and of course a Leading Engineering Officer of the Watch. My first decision was to get to know each of them. Immediately, I noticed that they each thought outside the box, a strength and a weakness. They also knew their performance shortfalls and wanted to get back on track. They came up with a plan that was thoughtful and cutting edge enough to—in a few specifics—scare me. They were also very experienced personnel, especially the enlisted. Their attitude was off the charts. I was their leader and had a role to play, central to which was making clear that improvement was going to have to be a team effort. I trusted their experience and expertise, and after making just a few minor adjustments to Crew A's plan, it became OUR plan.

After three months, our performance skyrocketed. We had the best performing students—officer and enlisted—and were considered the best performing crew at the facility. Our success was traceable not to leader or follower, but to: clarity of purpose, total commitment, high standards, joint trust, the importance of relationships, and the courage to forge ahead.

It was neither the first nor the last time I experienced a team in swing during my years in the U.S. Navy. It is an experience encapsulated in the dynamic between coxswain Bobby Moch and stroke Don Hume during their 1936 Olympic eights race. Moch and Hume perfectly illustrate the difference-maker dynamic under pressure.[2]

In that race, stroke Don Hume rowed in the stroke seat even though he was very sick. Behind by a full five seconds, Bobby Moch pleaded with Hume to take the stroke higher. Nothing happened. Hume seemed completely out of it, his head rocking back and forth to the rhythm of the boat. Moch couldn't make eye contact with Hume. He fought off panic. Daniel Brown picks up the play-by-play in *The Boys in the Boat*,

> Bobby Moch was still desperately trying to figure out what to do. Hume still wasn't responding, as they approached the twelve-hundred-meter mark, the situation was becoming critical. The only option Moch had left, the only thing he could think of, was to hand the stroke off to Joe. It would be a dangerous move—unheard of, really—more likely than not to confuse everyone with an oar in his hand, to throw

the rhythm of the boat into utter chaos. But Moch had lost his ability to regulate the pace of his boat, and that spelled certain doom.

As Moch leaned forward to tell Joe to set the stroke and raise the rate, Don Hume's head snapped up, his eyes popped open, he clamps his mouth shut, and he looked Bobby Moch straight in the eyes. Moch, startled, locked his eyes with him and yelled, "Pick'er up! Pick'er up!" Hume picked up the pace.[3]

There is a mystical connection of affection between the leader and the follower when inspiration merges with trust in a high performing team. Moch and Hume went on to win by .6 seconds over Germany and Italy for the Olympic Gold medal. Leadership is about followership and followership is about leadership. This is the relational connection that moves teams. It is the difference-maker dynamic.

# CHAPTER 5

---

# A PERSON
# TO FOLLOW

*Pocock believed that rowing was the finest builder of char-
acter of any sport, involving as it does the most rigorous discipline, greatest endurance, intense concentration, and total
self-control. He saw in it the basis for success in most areas
of human endeavor—a willingness to pool one's strength in
a common cause.*

— GORDON NEWELL [1]

*The Virtue Proposition* puts front and center what every leadership book touches on, but all too often shies from acknowledging explicitly. A leader must be a person worth following.
A person's worth cannot be measured without accounting for
her or his character, and when the stakes are highest, only
a virtuous character is worth following. Technical competence is requisite, but it does not speak to trust, or integrity,
or courage. Virtuous leaders participate in something spiritual
that is visible in their conduct. They are identifiable by the

transparent exercise of practices that reflect the application of virtue to their behavior. It is within everyone's capabilities.

Every great leader was, and remains, a follower. You learn how to live from somebody else. It is a sign of maturity when you become aware of whom you have been following and can evaluate the results of their teachings on your life. A person's character is shaped by their commitment to timeless transcendent virtues, which is further inspired by the life of someone who they follow. Parents, teachers, coaches, religious leaders, and peers all present themselves as individuals who might be worth following. But there is also value in reading the biographies of great men and women.

The leadership model of this book is based on character, based on a timeless and transcendent set of core virtues, and a passion to serve others before self. In the next several chapters, we turn from the preparation for leadership to the principles required by it.

These principles are found in the writings of Greek philosophers and Roman statesmen (e.g., Plato, Sophocles, and Cicero), early Christian theologians (e.g., Augustine, Aquinas, Catherine of Siena, Luther, and Erasmus), Enlightenment and Transcendentalist thinkers (e.g., Adam Smith, Margaret Fuller, Frederick Douglass, and Henry David Thoreau), and modern-day writers such as James MacGregor Burns, Dietrich Bonhoeffer, Barbara Kellerman, Bill George, Ira Chaleff, Patrick Lencioni, and Robert Greenleaf. All emphasize the importance of embodying universal ethical principles.

Robert Greenleaf coined the phrase "servant leadership" in his 1970 essay, "The Servant as Leader."[2] The servant leader makes sure that other people's highest-priority needs are being served. Greenleaf writes, "The best test, and difficult to administer, is: do those served grow as persons? Do they, while being served, become healthier, wiser, freer, more autonomous, more likely themselves to become servants?"

The leadership model of this book assumes the significance of servant leadership.

Over the years, qualities of servant leadership have been demonstrated in the lives of many individuals past and present, known and unknown. William Wilberforce, Mother Teresa, Nelson Mandela, Martin Luther King Jr., Dalai Lama, Abraham Lincoln, Harriet Tubman, George C. Marshall, Dietrich Bonhoeffer, Helmut von Moltke, Mahatma Gandhi, Albert Schweitzer, Ida B. Wells, Cesar Chavez, Oskar Schindler, Desmond Tutu, and Thurgood Marshall—all lived lives in exemplary service to others.

This aspiration of serving others is shared by all cultures and religious traditions. All the major world religions—Buddhism, Hinduism, Islam, Taoism, Judaism, and Christianity—have versions of the Golden Rule. C. S. Lewis goes further to state, "What is common to them all . . . is the doctrine of objective value, the belief that certain attitudes are really true, and others really false, to the kind of thing the universe is and the kind of things we are."[3] There are timeless, transcendent virtues that are rooted in the way the world works. Once embraced, they act on character as gravity does on all matter. It is within everyone's capabilities to embrace these virtues.[4]

A common adage in rowing is to keep your "mind in the boat" (M-I-B). This means in the thick of a race, every oarsman's full concentration must be on the rower in front of her. Any side glance will upset the rhythm to disastrous results. To be distracted is to lose the rhythm, catch a crab, disrupt the entire team. The shared trust, love, and commitment to excellence is what allows them to see only the rower in front. To keep one's head in the boat is to embrace fully this shared commitment. Similarly, to embrace the gravity of behavior attuned to virtues is what makes this possible for leaders and teams.

My understanding of servant leadership demands commitment to living by—and developing within yourself and among others—five virtues: love, integrity, truth, excellence, and relationships. We now turn to describing them more fully.

## Love

The injunction to love thy neighbors is shared by all major world religions and exemplified by every noble leader. When Jesus was asked what the most important commandment was, he answered, "The most important of all the commandments is this: 'The Lord Yahweh, our God, is one! You are to love the Lord Yahweh, your God, with a passionate heart, from the depths of your soul, with your every thought, and with all your strength. This is the great and supreme command. And the second is this: 'You must love your neighbor in the same way you love yourself.' You will never find a greater commandment than these" (Mark 12:29-31). Jesus made love the touchstone of both belief and behavior.

When Jesus spoke of love, he was not talking about a feeling, but a mindset, a lifestyle. He used the Greek word *agape* to describe love. This word is about actions and behavior. Love in this sense is self-sacrificing, serving, and giving. It treats others as we would like to be treated. It walks the walk. Jesus summarized a tenet found in every major religion as follows: "Do to others as you would have them do to you."

At an even deeper level, Jesus suggests that you become whatever you love. It becomes the controlling, determinative variable in your life. The question of love is not simply how you treat other people, but more profoundly what you long for. The answer to this question will shape the arc of your life. Or put differently, your life arc will reveal your answer to this question: Are empathy, connection, and care for others the determinative longings of your life?

A person worth following, a person followers can embrace as a leader and a mentor, is someone who can answer yes to those questions. Values-based leaders can get you only so far. Only virtues-based leaders can deliver teams that sustain excellence over time. This is possible when excellence is supported by love, integrity, truth, and emotionally intelligent relationships.

Rabbi Jonathan Sacks, the late British Orthodox Rabbi, and former Chief Rabbi of the United Hebrew Congregations of the Commonwealth, underscores the generative nature of love,

> The more friendship I share, the more I have. The more love I give, the more I possess. The best way to learn something is to teach it to others. The best way to have influence is to share it as widely as possible. These are the things that operate by the logic of multiplication not division, and they are precisely what is created and distributed in communities of faith: friendship, love, learning, and moral influence, along with those many other things which exist by virtue of being shared.[5]

A person of any faith, or of none, can recognize that Jesus of Nazareth's life demonstrated the impact he had on others. His compassion, courage, character, and his ability to touch lives turned a small rag-tag group of followers into a worldwide force for good that has influenced generations. If leadership is defined as a "relationship of influence," or the ability to attract followers, then Jesus satisfied both criteria.

The virtue of love was central to the life of Jesus, but it did not exist in isolation. When one examines the life of Jesus, you also see the other four virtues: integrity, truth, excellence, and relationships.

## Integrity

Integrity is living out what you claim to be important to you. A measure of our current crisis in leadership is how rarely contemporary leaders invoke integrity to explain their choices, their accomplishments, their lives. While the importance of integrity is felt daily—from interactions with your auto mechanic to your delegation to a colleague a time-sensitive task—full expression of its role in leadership behavior is best found in older texts. From Stoic philosophers to the prophets of the world's dominant faiths, we find the clearest expression of integrity's importance to behavior worth following.

For example, Jesus's message was a call to live a life of integrity:

> The eye is the lamp of the body. So, if your eye is healthy, you whole body will be full of light, but if your eye is bad,

your whole body will be full of darkness. If then the light in you is darkness, how great is the darkness! (Matthew 6:22)

You are the salt of the earth, but if salt has lost its taste, how shall its saltiness be restored? It is no longer good for anything except to be thrown out and trampled under people's feet. (Matthew 5:13)

An even older example is found in *Meditations*, the writings of Marcus Aurelius, the philosopher and ruler of Rome. There he put it succinctly: "A man should be upright, not kept upright."[6]

As a leader are you a purveyor of light or a dispenser of darkness? Are you salt that has lost all its taste? There is probably no greater basis for authenticity in your leadership than whether you walk the walk with consistency and integrity.

## Truth

Jesus wanted people to examine themselves and the world around them. He called people to live their lives aligned with reality. He is often quoted, "You will know the truth, and the truth will set you free." (John 8:32) The truth does not set one free in the sense of letting you live your life any way that you want. The freedom here is a life aligned to the gravitational reality of virtues, and a life so aligned enables you to flourish. All leaders start with the responsibility to examine their characters and thereafter understand their alignment to reality. This is a commitment to the virtue of truth.

Do you know who you are and who you are not? Do you recognize not only your strengths but also your shortcomings?

How true are the ideas that shape your worldview? Are you blinded by your own ambitions, false hopes, or fictitious stories about the good life? What does the arc of your life look like? What do you leave in your wake? Are you shackled to the past or pulled forward by the future? When the storms of life come, and they always do, will the foundation of your life hold? Jesus warned,

> Everyone then who hears these words of mind *and does them* will be like a wise man who built his house on the rock. And the rains fell, and the floods came, and the winds blew and beat on the house, but it did not fall, because it had been founded on the rock. And everyone who hears these words of mind and *does not do them* will be like a foolish man who built his house on the sand. And the rain fell, and the floods came, and the winds blew and beat against the house, and it fell, and great was the fall of it. (Matthew 7:24-27)

An authentic life must be built on something. Is that something a firm foundation or merely shifting sand? Does it have the consistency of truth, or the variability of feeling? Every life is a clear answer to this question. For Jesus, truth is the only thing that will set you free. For teams, it is prerequisite for achieving excellence.

## Excellence

Does your daily conduct reflect the virtues of love, integrity, and truth? William Wilberforce spent over forty years fighting for England's abolition of slavery. He inspired friends and colleagues who likewise took up the cause. It was a lifelong struggle. He died in 1833, three days before Britain passed the Slavery Abolition Act, and a year before its implementation. That he did not live to witness the Act's passage had no bearing on the excellence of Wilberforce's efforts. They were derived from practice. Excellence is the fruit of a disciplined lifestyle and a consistent journey.

Excellence can also be achieved through learning from failure. It is a false expectation that we will never make mistakes. The key is the willingness to learn from them, to use them as a motivation for continued commitment to excellence.

This experience of stumbling and getting up again has a purpose—the pursuit of excellence. A person motivated by love and a seeker of truth realizes the inner need to change, learn, and grow. Excellence is a lifelong journey of becoming authentic: a person of character, conduct marked by integrity, and a calling marked by a clear sense of purpose. The goal is to become a difference-maker for the common good. As in most worthwhile journeys, the road is never easy.

## Relationships

When a commitment to love, integrity, truth, and excellence are combined, forging relationships becomes an inevitable priority. Jesus knew who he was. He understood his purpose and stated it boldly. In his hometown of Nazareth, he stood up and proclaimed the words of Isaiah as applying to himself.

> The Spirit of the Lord is upon me, because he has anointed me, to proclaim good news to the poor. He has sent me

to proclaim liberty to the captives and recovering of sight to the blind, to set at liberty those who are oppressed, to proclaim the year of the Lord's favor. (Luke 4:18)

His life was focused on bringing "favor" or a purposeful life to people. He called people to join him, spent time with them, taught them, held them accountable to be people of actionable compassion.

His ability to develop healthy relationships with people of varying backgrounds, beliefs, and perspectives—particularly those consciously marginalized by his society—empowered his leadership. He lived and worked with ordinary people and treated each of them with respect. Though he listened, he often responded by asking insightful, probing questions. When asked, "Who is my neighbor?" he answered, "Anyone you happen to come upon each day who has a specific need you can meet, particularly those others ignore."

Surprisingly we typically do not effectively measure the relational skills of leaders. And yet, it is in their absence where most conflicts arise. To be an effective teacher, a person needs competent mastery of their field as well as consistent connectivity with his or her students. In most cases, the barrier to high performance teams stems from relational connectivity rather than either the leader's or the followers' sufficient technical mastery. The legacy of your life, particularly in your relationships, is worth the effort.

Jesus gave definition to the virtues he embodied, the virtues of love, integrity, truth, excellence, and relationships. He was a beacon of decency, civility, goodness, a new day, and meaningful life. His presence made the lives of those all around him better. He led from the front, but with humility. History has shown that such a life makes a difference.

Rabbi Sacks summarizes this:

> What then is society? It is where we set aside all considerations of wealth and power and value people for what they are and what they give. It is where Jew and Christian, Muslim and Hindu, Buddhist and Sikh can come together, bound by their commonalities, enlarged by their differences. It is where we join in civil conversation about the kind of society we wish to create for the sake of our grandchildren not yet born. It is where we share an overarching identity, a first language of citizenship, despite our different second languages of ethnicity or faith. It is where strangers can become friends. It is not a vehicle of salvation, but it is the most effective form yet devised for respectful coexistence. Society is the home we build together when we bring our several gifts to the common good.[7]

While profound, servant leadership as exemplified in figures across human history is humble and well within the abilities of all of us. Indeed, it is rare that we live lives without ever encountering it. I was lucky enough to first discover such leadership as a child.

After my father hit a professional reversal in the late 1950s, he receded into his thoughts and alcohol. Neither combative nor mean, he simply spent hours of each day in his chair, reading, or asleep. My mother stepped up. So, too, did neighbors.

My mother did everything she could to make ends meet, attended school and sporting events, and made sure my brother and I never doubted her love for and faith in us. When I fell behind in third grade, it was Mrs. Gladys Ritchie who spent the extra hours to open my world to reading. And at twelve, I began working for Joe Koenig, the owner of a small grocery and butcher store a few blocks away from my home. I stocked shelves, mowed his lawn, even carried his store's cash earnings to the bank for deposit. My wages went to the family income, an occasional baseball mitt for me. Aware of my family's difficulties, Mr. Koenig would on occasion send me home with a T-bone steak for dinner. He took me to an occasional Detroit Tigers baseball game. He could be tough, but he knew what love was and he showed it every day.

Servant leadership is the foundation for authentic leadership—upon which everything else is built. Servant leadership is not the abdication of leadership, but the proactive effort toward creating the conditions that enable swing. It is not about a style of leadership but becoming the kind of person with an established character that is reflected in a consistent set of behaviors that fosters the flourishing of others. Practiced within and among teams, servant leadership becomes generative of truth, integrity, love, excellence, and relationships.

A leader worth following exemplifies these virtues. What is more, she instills and encourages these virtues among her team members. No matter the team's performance goal, a leader of competence and virtues allows her team to keep their "heads in the boat," focused on the tasks at hand, knowing that the way forward is guided by love, truth, integrity, excellence, and valued relationships—and the courage to do so. The more demanding and change-making the goal, the more essential such a leader becomes.

# CHAPTER 6

## THE HEART OF A TEAM

*George Pocock learned much about the hearts and souls of young men. He learned to see hope where a boy thought there was no hope, to see skill where skill was obscured by ego or by anxiety. He observed the fragility of confidence and the redemptive power of trust. He detected the strength of the gossamer threads of affection that sometimes grew between a pair of young men or among a boatload of them striving honestly to do their best. And he came to understand how those almost mystical bonds of trust and affection, if nurtured correctly, might lift a crew above the ordinary sphere, transport it to a place where nine boys somehow became one thing.*

— **DANIEL JAMES BROWN**[1]

A leader worth following is grounded by his adherence to core virtues that are expressed in conduct that demonstrates his virtue intelligence. This is visible in conduct reflecting an emotional intelligence aligned with his virtues and ability to lead.

Every team has an evolving emotional core. If the team is to achieve greatness, it begins with it achieving emotional swing as well as technical swing. This is only possible with a leader who exhibits virtue intelligence. Herein lies the potential heart of the team. The character of a leader is experienced by the team through his or her virtue intelligence. This is perhaps the most overlooked aspect of a leader's development and yet it is essential when leadership is applied to a team. Emotional intelligence is not a new concept, having received attention by scholars and business leaders for years. Virtue intelligence is likewise not new, but it has been buried of late by the 20th century's fixation on scientific data and rationalism at any cost.

In rowing, coaches can become fixated on two-kilometer erg times and bench press and leg lift numbers. This attention to detail, while valuable, is not enough for a high performance team. In companies, executives and board members and market-watch critics can become fixated on profits, valuations, and share values. This profit-loss attention to bottom-line detail, while valuable, is not enough for high performance teams. In both cases, the relational intangibles matter. To realize high performance, the emotional connections, mutual affection, and irrevocable trust in one another loom to the forefront of performance considerations. For companies it is under conditions of extreme deadlines, demanding exactitude in deliverables, competition for materials or markets where these factors make the decisive difference. For rowers, it is under conditions of extreme personal pain, physical exhaustion, and intense competition where margins of victory are measured in hundredths of a second that these factors make the decisive difference.

The idea of emotional intelligence or "EQ" first appeared in Daniel Goleman's 1995 book, *Emotional Intelligence: Why It Can Matter More than IQ.*[2] Since then, extensive research has been done on the concept both comparing emotional intelligence to intellectual intelligence as well as assessing its benefits to actual teams, organizations, and companies.

What many had intuited by anecdotal experience was confirmed by Goleman. IQ and the other reductive measures of school achievement do not predict success in life or leadership. In fact, when compared side by side, high IQ predicts on average 6 percent of success whereas EQ is directly responsible for between 27 and 45 percent of job success.[3] Overall effective leadership demands proficiency in three things: technical skills, cognitive abilities, and emotional intelligence. Of these three categories, emotional intelligence proved to be twice as important as the others for performance success. In senior leadership, the difference between a star performer and an average performer was 90 percent attributable to emotional intelligence. Effective team performance is dependent upon the application of emotional intelligence. Excellent team performance is dependent upon the application of virtue intelligence.

Emotional intelligence is the heart of a team. Virtue intelligence is its soul. We start from the heart, and work to the soul.

What are the building blocks of emotional intelligence? According to Steven Stein and Howard Book in *The EQ Edge: Emotional Intelligence and Your Success,* "Emotional intelligence is made up of short-term, tactical, dynamic skills which can be brought into play as the situation warrants and can be improved by means of training, coaching, and experience."[4] There are several models of emotional intelligence. The model advanced here is based on Multi-Health Systems, Inc. It includes an assessment of the five building blocks of emotional and social functioning: Self-Perception, Self-Expression, Interpersonal, Decision-Making, and Stress Management.

## Self-Perception

Self-perceptions include the leader's ability to know and manage himself or herself. Such self-awareness means having a deep understanding of one's emotions, strengths, weaknesses, needs, and drives. The goal here is to have an honest and realistic assessment of oneself—one that is neither too critical nor too confident.

## Self-Expression

Self-expression deals with the way a leader faces the world. It balances one's assertiveness and independence with one's vulnerability and openness. Such a balance enhances whether people perceive you as authentic and approachable.

## Interpersonal

The interpersonal includes the leaders' people skills—how they interact and get along with others. This has three parts:

1. Ability to make and maintain relationships
2. Degree of empathy towards others, and
3. Ability to exercise social responsibility to society at large

Since leadership is grounded in followership and the mutual sharing of inspiration and trust, influence and purpose, the importance of interpersonal relationship skills is self-evident. Your ability to give and receive trust and compassion and to establish and maintain mutually satisfying personal relationships is pivotal to leadership success.

## Decision-Making

Decision-making involves the leaders' ability to use emotions in the best way to solve problems. Notice that this skill is *not* simply about solving problems, but the ability to solve problems in a manner that takes the emotional context of others into consideration. This also has three parts:

1. Impulse control
2. Reality testing, and
3. Problem-solving

It is most often in the decision-making process that the leader's commitment to returning authority, embracing ambiguity, and maintaining empathy when there are differences of opinion or overt conflict are most revealed.

## Stress Management

Stress management has to do with being flexible, tolerant, and able to control your impulses. Under the conditions of crew racing, the ability to maintain focus and equanimity under pressure is an obvious advantage. The ability to maintain a realistically positive attitude in the face of adversity is a major strength.

The composite attitude when these other variables are addressed is happiness, a general satisfaction with life. When people obtain this, they bring a zest for living into the workplace and the team.

Emotional intelligence is not the same thing as personality. Like IQ, personality is fixed and static. This enables personality tests to divide people into types. In contrast, emotional intelligence is not a static category but a dynamic one. It is always found on an evolving continuum involving strengths and weaknesses. Consequently, emotional intelligence allows for growth and change, particularly through training, coaching, and life experience.

An additional factor that should be considered when assessing one's strengths and weaknesses within emotional intelligence is that in isolation a single attribute can be taken to an extreme. Too much self-regard can be viewed as arrogance. Too much self-actualization can lead to self-centeredness. Too much emotional self-awareness can cause hypersensitivity, and so on. Each of these factors needs to be assessed and balanced with all the others. Additionally, they need to be understood in the immediate context in which they are being implemented. Each team member needs to aspire to, and work toward, emotional harmony as well as technical competence.

This balancing act is where emotional intelligence can tip over and into virtue intelligence. Neither EQ nor VQ can be assessed alone, which leads to behavioral blind spots. Awareness of your EQ and VQ is only achieved in a trusting community and with the accountability of a trusted mentor.

Moreover, because new emotional habits and behaviors need to be developed, this mentoring and accountability needs to be carried out over time within real life experiences. It is through the process of mentored practice that emotional intelligence can be elevated into virtue intelligence. This has been the real-time experience of the Severn Leadership Group's five-month program. This program begins with a personal emotional intelligence assessment. Thereafter, a cohort of other leaders can move beyond theory to implementing these ideas into an individual's sphere of influence and team. Eventually, attention is given to a leader's character and consequent conduct. As a leader's behavior becomes ever more consistent, her virtue intelligence is assessed and strengthened.

This is why VQ cannot be developed by good intentions alone. A stronger motivator than intentions or will is needed. It needs to be attachment.

Because attachment is relational, attachment grows in the context of our connections to other people. Minimally, the leader's attachment to his or her mentor is critical. But even more decisive is the leader's attachment to his other team members. When an individual is attached by affection, empathy, and love with others on his or her team, the identity of each individual, as expressed in desired and worked-for outcomes, merges with the team identity. When this happens, it forms the strongest and mutually reinforcing linkage between the leader and the other team members. The individual's identity and the group's identity experience a synchronicity of emotional alignment or emotional swing. The deepest force that creates human character is relational and can only be forged through the experience of teamwork. In the end, we become who we love and who we love serves as the strongest motivator for our changed behavior. At this level, swing is rooted in and animated by love.

Most ex-oarsmen will tell you that they learned more fundamentally important lessons about life in the racing shell than in the classroom. This is the relational forge—where character is developed, and first emotional intelligence followed by virtue intelligence is learned.

## Linking EQ Behaviors to Virtue

The tendency to think of EQ in terms of amorphous feelings encourages the misstep of evaluating progress by behavior instead of by conduct. Simply put, a behavior is what you did on a particular Monday; conduct is what you aspire to demonstrate every day throughout your life. The difference between the terms is captured in the fact that the United States Uniform Code of Military Justice speaks to Conduct Unbecoming, not Behavior Unbecoming. Conduct reflects matters of honesty, decency, fairness, justice, and decorum. It reflects virtues. Evaluating behavior, not conduct, is a mistake that makes it impossible to evaluate progress and make constructive relational change. Evaluating conduct is what allows for evaluating virtue intelligence. This is because virtues are not based in feelings. Nor is VQ. It is expressed in consistent conduct. This can be seen by overlapping the leadership virtues—love, integrity, truth, excellence, and relationships (LITER)—with the behavioral components of the EQ-i2.0 model.[5] When five virtues are compared to the fifteen aspirational behaviors of EQ-i2.0, the following nine leadership priorities emerge:

## Interpersonal

- Interpersonal relationships
- Empathy
- Social responsibility

## Self-Expression

- Assertiveness
- Independence
- Problem-solving

## The Big Three

- Self-regard
- Self-actualization
- Optimism

Because they are backstopped by transcendent virtues, these priorities animate the conduct of virtuous leaders and virtuous organizations. In this insight rests the possibility for transformational growth, change, and difference-making. This is why it is important that leaders work with mentors on the behaviors that, based on an EQ-i2.0 assessment, need strengthening to better align with their code of conduct.

The following Leadership Model describes these relationships.

# Leadership Model

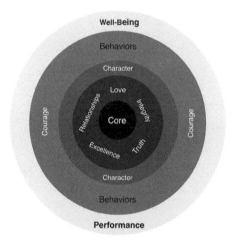

## EQ-i Behaviors

| | | |
|---|---|---|
| Self-Regard | Interpersonal | Assertiveness |
| Self-Actualization | Relationships Empathy | Independence |
| Optimism | Social Responsibility | Problem-Solving |

Within the overlapping, interconnected, reinforcing qualities of the Leadership Model is visible the power of virtue intelligence when it is at the heart of a successful team. For it is only with self-awareness, balance, and synchronicity that a team can meaningfully amp up the performance threshold to serve an attachment bond that transcends individual intention or motivation.

This is the core dynamic of every effective team, though it is frequently overlooked. When Bobby Moch looked into the eyes of Don Hume at the close of the 1936 Olympic gold medal race, and yelled, "Pick'er up! Pick'er up!" this is the unconscious neurological dynamic that kicked in, an affection-animated emotional swing born of an aligned emotional intelligence between coxswain and stroke.

It was virtue intelligence, however, that differentiated that medal-winning team. Coach Al Ulbrickson put his finger on this fact when he observed, "Every man in the boat had absolute confidence in every one of his mates. . . . Why they won cannot be attributed to individuals, not even the stroke of Don Hume. Heartfelt cooperation all spring was responsible for the victory."[6] It is the mystical relational experience that only teamwork under pressure can meaningfully provide. Virtue intelligence is the leadership core of effective teams.

In their analysis of success and EQ, Stein and Book conclude, "It seems likely that emotionally intelligent players are more likely to have the staying power that leads to success as an athlete. This is something that professional coaches, scouts, and trainers in all areas of sport should take note of."[7] Virtue intelligence is essential for swing. Indeed, another word for the experience of swing is joy, an overwhelming satisfaction with the process of living—to be able to embrace all aspects of life with cheerfulness and enthusiasm. Such teams have a magnetic attractiveness to others because belonging to something larger than oneself while being affirmed in one's own individual contribution is what we long for.

# CHAPTER 7

## THE PARADOX OF LEADERSHIP

The paradox of leadership is that it is not about the leader. Put simply, a leader cannot truly become an effective leader without the investment of others in his or her life and reciprocally, in the lives of his or her team. Swing is mutually dependent on leaders and followers, for without others genuine connection is not possible. And it is in the connection that true leadership is found.

Connection fueled by virtue intelligence is much easier to achieve in theory or on paper. It is much more difficult in real life. We all come to our work or to our teams with our life experiences and wounds. Such was certainly the case of Joe Rantz.

Joe Rantz's mother died of throat cancer when he was five. Two years later, his father married a woman seventeen years his junior. Three children later, Joe's stepmother Thula became alienated from Joe. Daniel Brown writes, "So began Joe's life in exile. Thula would no longer cook for him, so every morning before school and again every evening he trudged down the wagon road to the cookhouse at the bottom of the mountain to work for the company cook, Mother Cleveland, in exchange for breakfast and dinner . . . He fed himself and made his way, but his world had grown dark, narrow, and lonely. There were no boys his age whom he could befriend in the camp."[1]

Connection for Rantz was a foreign concept and a distant reality. The same can be said of many leaders. Initially, leaders who pride themselves on their technical knowledge find their work world juxtaposed to their home life where connection is self-evidently needed. But soon leaders realize that relational connection is just as essential to their work world as well, particularly in building effective teams. This is because connection is the essence of the human experience. What gets a person on a team is not always what makes them an effective team member.

Connection demands closer inspection of both the individual and the team. What fosters the potential for human connection? This question is explored by Joseph Luft and Harry Ingham in a four-paned window, which divides personal awareness into four different types, as represented by its four quadrants: Open, Hidden, Blind, and Unknown.[2]

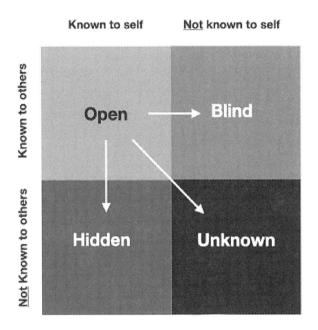

The Open quadrant represents things that you know about yourself and that people know about you. For example, you know your name and so do your colleagues and friends. Most will know some of your interests and family information. The knowledge in the Open quadrant can include not only information but feelings, motives, behaviors, wants, needs, and desires. Indeed, it can include any information that describes who you are. When you first meet a new person, the information held in this quadrant is not very large since there has been little time to exchange information.

In teams and working groups, a goal should be the development and expansion of the open area for every person, because when this area is expanded, people are more effective and productive. The open quadrant minimizes distortions and mistrust by providing opportunities for dialogue on topics that are acknowledged as important.

My most bracing experience with this invitation to disclose myself was offered to me by Admiral Hyman Rickover, the Navy's Director of Nuclear Reactors from 1949 to 1982 and the father of the United States' nuclear navy. He was responsible for every aspect of developing, constructing, and operating the Navy's nuclear fleet. He was an engineer's engineer: demanding and irascible. He also made it a point to interview every officer in his program, which in 1967 included me. After two Navy Captains had grilled me on my academics, my personal background, including my imminent marriage to Martha Harrison, who I intended to marry after graduating from the Naval Academy, I was ushered into Admiral Rickover's office. His plain wooden desk was strewn with papers. The chair I was put in had its two front legs shortened, pitching me at a downward angle facing him. He studied notes from the earlier interviews in silence.

He then looked up and said, "I see you are planning to get married after you graduate."

"Yes, sir."

A quick string of questions followed. What is her name, where does she go to school? And then, "I have a question for you. Can she cook?" Before I could reply, he continued. "Can she bake pies? What is your favorite pie?"

"Cherry—cherry pies, sir."

"Okay, okay. After you get married your wife bakes you a cherry pie. She puts it in front of you. You take a bite, and it tastes terrible. What are you going to do?"

Again, before I could even formulate an answer he continues.

"Here is what I want you to do. Stand up, pick up the pie, and tell her it is the worst pie you have ever tasted and then throw it on the floor. Will you do that for me and send me a letter when you have done it?"

I was quiet, but just for seconds, which was long enough for the Admiral to yell, "Will you do that?"

"No sir, I will not."

"Why? Why not?"

"That's not how to treat people. I would thank her for the pie, but indicate something was not quite right about it."

He looked at me for a second, stood and yelled, "Get out of here!"

The Admiral's interview techniques leave very much to be desired, but to this day I think in his inimitable manner, Rickover had found a question with which to fill up a good bit of the Open quadrant.

The key to an effective Open quadrant is providing the opportunity and encouraging the willingness for self-disclosure. Both require conscious effort. The challenge of realizing both is compounded when the team is functioning in a networked or virtual environment. This challenge should and can be transparently addressed.

The Hidden quadrant is where we keep the personal information that we do not want others to have access to. The reasons for keeping information hidden can range from it being sensitive, deeply personal facts that one does not want to share, to information that an employee would like to share, but does not feel there is adequate trust or safety to do so. In either of these situations, exposing hidden information to the team can have negative repercussions. However, if the organization is based on trust and respect, then sharing relevant hidden information which team members wish was in the Open quadrant, helps both the individual and the team.

Creating an emotional environment where this hidden information is safe to be shared is essential to creating an effective team. Connection requires creating a sense of belonging. What prevents connection is shame, which Admiral Rickover stepped dangerously close to invoking. To transcend shame requires vulnerability or allowing oneself to be known. The work of Dr. Brené Brown is salient. Her TED Talk, "The Power of Vulnerability," is now one of the top five most viewed TED Talks of all time.[3] Explaining the importance for effective teams to embrace vulnerability is why she has been brought in to counsel organizations as diverse as Microsoft, Pixar, and the Department of Defense. Allowing for vulnerability, to shift the Hidden to Open, does not happen without leaders willing and able to model vulnerability and teams willing and able to make this a priority. Great leaders lead with their weaknesses, not with their irascibility. Nothing creates a stronger sense of belonging, loyalty, and group cohesion than when a vulnerability is embraced.

It is the Blind quadrant that often holds the key to creating effective teams. This area involves information and behavior to which one is personally blind or unaware. When strengths and areas for development in this quadrant move into the Open quadrant, the recipient is better able to embrace changes that better serve the team. The blind spots identified in this area can range from technical competence to attitudinal issues. Regardless of the feedback shared here, it needs to be data that helps the recipient become a better team member. When this information is shared routinely it expands the open area and no one is exempt from participation. Unless feedback is a routine and regular part of a team's dynamic, a person can feel like they are being singled out or ganged up on. The Blue Angels, the flight demonstration squadron of the U.S. Navy, does a debrief and personal feedback session after every flight. In this case, regular feedback perfects performance and saves lives.

Ironically, it is the Unknown quadrant where the greatest potential for relational connection lies. The Unknown quadrant represents things that neither you nor others know about you. This quadrant taps into the fact that 95 percent of what motivates our behaviors stems from our unconscious mind. There is more that we don't know about ourselves—even when we are self-reflective—than we know. People are complex and much lies under the surface of our conscious minds. Shared living and events can surface feelings, thoughts, or interests that were never recognized before. These are instances where the Unknown area reveals clues to an inner life that has gone unnoticed. Recognizing these clues is important. They emerge over time through the experience of shared living, whether among family, friends, colleagues, or all three.

Today there is a clear distinction between your home life and your work. However, when we are talking about the issue of relational connection, these two overlap. Failure in one may well be indicative of failure in the other.

To summarize, 1) self-disclosure reduces the Hidden area, 2) allowing for vulnerability reduces the Hidden area, 3) regular feedback reduces the Blind area, and 4) the process of living together reduces the Unknown area. This is how connection is created both in the home and at work. In both places it is equally essential to the creation of an effective team.

When connection exists, the effects can be transformational for individuals and for teams.

"Joe was a good and popular student. His classmates found him outgoing, freewheeling, handy with a joke, and fun to be around. A few who got to know him better found that he could suddenly and unexpectedly turn somber—never nasty or hostile, but guarded, as if there was a part of him he didn't want you to touch."[4]

We all come to the necessity of connecting our lives and the wounds experienced therein to the world and the most important people in our lives. This was the reality of Joe Rantz. His mother had died when he was five. He had moved repeatedly during childhood. At fifteen he was abandoned by his family and learned to stoically survive alone. With steeled will and impressive resilience, he was selected to the first boat at the University of Washington rowing team. While the other boys headed to the shower, those selected to the first boat marched down to the lake for a celebratory row.

Daniel Brown continues,

At the north end of the lake, the coxswain called out, "Way... 'nuff!" The boys stopped rowing and the shell glided to a stop, the long oars trailing in the water alongside them. Dark clouds fringed with silver moonlight scudded by overhead, carried briskly along by the winds aloft. The boys sat without talking, breathing heavily, exhaling flumes of white breath. Even now that they had stopped rowing, their breathing was synchronized, and for a brief, fragile moment it seemed to Joe as if all of them were part of a single thing, something alive with breath and spirit of its own. . . . Joe gulped huge drafts of the frigid air and sat staring at the scene, watching it turn into a soft of colors as, for the first time since his family had left him, tears filled his eyes.

He turned his face to the water, fiddling with his oarlock so the others would not see. He didn't know where the tears had come from, what they were about. But something inside him had shifted, if only for a few moments.[5]

It was a connection that moved Rantz. He was now a part of a team, a new family, a living breathing thing larger than himself. He had an ever-widening opportunity to move the blind, the unknown, and the hidden out into the open. The paradox of leadership is that it is not about the leader. Even more, a leader cannot truly become an effective leader without the investment of others in his or her life. For without others willing to allow virtues to guide embracing trust, integrity, and love such that they are open to share, genuine connection is not possible. It is in conscious connection that true leadership is found.

For *The Virtue Proposition* the usefulness of Rantz's story is how it encapsulates the common experience of the paradox this chapter addresses. All of us have experienced being both follower and leader, of opening ourselves to others, allowing them to open to us, all to the purpose of accomplishing a shared goal. Within families this occurs commonly around birthdays, more memorably around weddings and funerals. Within organizations, this occurs commonly around routine accomplishments, the closing out of a quarter or the obtaining of a short-term sales objective, and more memorably around changes in leadership, ownership, strategic direction. Stories like Rantz's crystalize a circumstance immediately familiar to all of us, and with that familiarity the repeat experience of navigating it well or poorly, of encountering in ourselves and others the ability to open, disclose, respect the process of what remains blind and hidden, and what does not.

The promise of the virtue proposition is that the paradox of leadership is at once knowable, and resolvable, and the practices by which this is done go immediately to improved qualities of leadership and increased excellence of outcomes.

# CHAPTER 8

# THE PRICE OF LEVELING UP

*Crew races are not won by clones. They are won by crews, and great crews are carefully balanced blends of both physical abilities and personality types. . . . If they are going to row well together, each of these oarsmen must adjust to the needs and capabilities of the other. Each must be prepared to compromise something in the way of optimizing his stroke for the overall benefit of the boat. . . . Only in this way can the capabilities that come with diversity be turned to advantage rather than disadvantage.*

— DANIEL JAMES BROWN[1]

It is an idea at least as old as Euripides, the 400 BC Athenian playwright, who wrote, "Every man is like the company he is wont to keep."[2] For leaders and for followers, however, it is essential to know your team is not static. When the University of Washington coach Al Ulbrickson invited the legendary boat-builder George Pocock into the coach's launch, the boys in the boat knew that some changes to the lineup were inevitable. Though they weren't his words, Ulbrickson was seeking counsel from his resident-wise sage as to how best to level up his crew.

Marketing guru Seth Godin observed the following among a group that were asked to submit and share short biographies of themselves. If, after having had the opportunity to read each other's submissions, they are given the opportunity to update their bios, all the bios always get better. He concludes, "It's not because people didn't try the first time. It's because being surrounded by people on the same journey as you, causes you to level up." From this Godin arrives at the lesson hidden in Euripides' quote. "Your path forward," Godin writes, "is pretty simple: Decide on your journey and find some people who will cause you to level up."[3]

Effective teams don't just embrace diversity, they require it. Learning to discover, nurse, balance, and harness diversity for a common task is the mark of a great leader. How a leader does this is not luck; it's practice.

Balancing diversity in an organization as in a rowing shell requires listening, communication, and feedback. It demands an ongoing relational dynamic, which is central to *The Virtue Proposition*. This is not a book about leadership *per se*, but leadership in service to a team. That is why the book's governing metaphor is not rowing, but rowing an eight-person shell, which, including the coxswain and coach minimally, involves ten people. Put simply, the dynamics of team leadership cannot be learned in a single shell, but only in a rowing eight. Similarly, a team leader can only be formed in the presence of and with the involvement of other people. The making of a team leader is a collaborative task.

Having examined the character and attitudes one needs to become a leader, and having introduced the attributes required of virtuous leaders, we turn to the process of becoming a leader, a process that requires sustained accountability. Tragically, most corporate leaders give the idea lip service before doing all they can to distance themselves from accountability.

Writing in the *Harvard Business Review*, Ron Carucci noted in 2020 that "data shows that 82% of managers acknowledge they have 'limited to no' ability to hold others accountable successfully, and 91% of employees would say that 'effectively holding others accountable' is one of their company's top leadership-development needs."[4] The consequences of so little meaningful accountability are visible everywhere around us, from the failures among America's current leaders all the way down to the experiences of the American worker. Carucci cites data showing that only 14 percent of employees "feel their performance is managed in a way that motivates them," and a whopping 69 percent "don't feel they're living up to their potential at work."

Bluntly, Americans are unhappy at work: tension, boredom, and apathy prevail. The Gallup poll indicates that 49 percent of the workforce is not engaged, and 14 percent are totally disengaged. Taken together this means that at any one time roughly two-thirds of the team are not consciously involved in fulfilling the team's mission. Recently, the trend of "quiet quitting" has emerged. Quiet quitting refers to doing the minimum requirements of one's job and putting in no more time, effort, or enthusiasm than absolutely necessary. According to a Gallup survey of workers age eighteen and older taken in June 2022, quiet quitters "make up at least 50% of the U.S. workforce—probably more." The percentage is particularly high among workers underage thirty-five, Gallup reported.[5]

In a rowing eight, if six of the oarsmen are not engaged, it is unlikely that the crew will leave the starting line much less finish a race. And yet, that level of apathy and lack of engagement, with the consequent performance, is routinely accepted in most organizations and places of business. It is the norm, not the exception. The opposite of what Ulbrickson, Pocock, and Godin are focused on—leveling up—occurs routinely. Most teams are actively leveling down.

The experience of disappointed disengagement is heightened among younger workers, such as millennials, who have an even higher set of expectations about their work experience. They want their work to have meaning and purpose. They want to use their talents and strengths to do what they do best every day. They want to learn and develop. They want their job to fit their life, or more accurately to blend more fully with their identity. Instead, they find dysfunctional organizations blended with toxic leaders.

Virtuous leaders actively encouraging teams to level up is the solution.

An organization is healthy when its culture, purpose, strategy, leadership, and followership fit together in an inclusive, consistent way. Such organizations are identifiable by the questions, explicit and implicit, being asked repeatedly. Are people engaged or merely putting in their time? Do people trust each other? Is there a collective sense of purpose and enduring standard of excellence? Do people feel they are valued and are making a difference?

Such an organizational dynamic does not happen by accident. Nor does it happen automatically. It necessitates input from a leader. The leader sets the tone for her team.

On the one hand, an authentic leader inspires, encourages, and develops each member of her team and, in so doing, betters the team. Team members know their backs are covered. They have support and will not be hung out to dry if something does not go as planned. Every person counts and is counted on.

On the other hand, an inauthentic leader can be toxic. The team's purpose or mission is vague. Roles and responsibilities are not clearly defined. Communication is infrequent, along with useful feedback. Micromanagement is often the order of the day. Results are less than expected and one's work is reduced to merely a job.

Team members deserve a leader who inspires, who leads by example. A fast way to ascertain whether or not they have such a leader is to judge the team.

A healthy organization or team is one that displays:

- Clarity of purpose
- An engaged workforce
- High morale
- High retention rates
- Clear communication
- Constructive feedback, and
- Openness to learning

A healthy organization breeds high performance, defined as the ability to deliver meaningful, measurable, and financially sustainable results for the people and causes the organization is in existence to serve.

To accomplish this, the leader within the organization needs a structural roundtable. The roundtable of Camelot fame offers a useful metaphor. Most organizations are only comprised of a king and an assortment of noble knights. Critically missing are Merlin, the wise sage, and Dagonet, the court jester. Most organizations surround their leaders with yes men: men who are unwilling or fearful of providing critical feedback. The consequences are most visible when a leader ends the practice. For example, college president Steven B. Sample—the man who turned the University of Southern California into one of the most respected and highly rated universities in the country—did so by advocating for contrarian leadership, an organizational structure that championed contrarian perspectives. This is what Merlin and Dagonet provide. The first by virtue of his wisdom and experience. The second by virtue of personal critical observations that, given with humor, reveals the king's blind spots. If these two roles are not built into the culture of an organization, then trust and inspiration—the key to the leadership/followership dynamic—are forfeited. There is wisdom to be found in Camelot.[6]

Two areas are particularly indicative of an effective roundtable or healthy organization: feedback and micromanaging. The former inspires leveling up. The latter guarantees leveling down.

## Feedback

Constructive feedback involves discussions about performance, strengths, and areas for growth. Project performance is explicit and frank, focused on where things went well and which areas need improving. The same goes for overall team performance, including strengths and areas that need further attention. It is essential that this feedback go in both directions, from the team to the leader and from the leader to the team.

Open communication has two additional benefits. First, it helps to improve overall performance. Issues are identified and resolved early, even before they become problems. When individual and team performance is reviewed, people have an opportunity to reflect on their work, make changes, and revise plans that ultimately result in improved results and greater personal satisfaction.

Second, open communication creates opportunities for honest and frank dialogue. It is important for the discussions to be specific, not generalized, so that the leader gets to know his people on a deeper level. How can we improve? What's lurking around the corner? Holding your cards closely and not saying what needs to be said undermines an effective team. When people feel they are in an environment where their input is valued and taken seriously, seeds of trust are planted, and extraordinary teams begin to bloom.

In her article, "How to Give Your Team Feedback," Rebecca Knight makes the following recommendations:

1. **Set expectations early**—It is less about being an approachable leader than it is about having feedback routinely structured into every aspect of the organization.
2. **Ask general questions**—Create a safe environment where honesty and candor are rewarded.
3. **Work your way up to structured reviews**—Once a general expectation that everything is going to be subject to a debrief and a feedback review has been established, you can then structure more formal reviews. Until the culture of feedback is formed, the more formal structured reviews will not achieve the desired results.
4. **Keep performance issues out in the open**—The management mantra, "Praise in public, criticize in private," does not serve well in team settings. When teams have problems, feedback should all be out in the open.
5. **Foster team relationships**—Conflict within a team is inevitable, so encourage the team to resolve these conflicts themselves.
6. **Debrief every project**—Something can be learned about performance after every team effort, so encourage the team to realize that they are being reviewed not simply as individuals but as a team.[7]

A team leader intent on leveling up through feedback needs to adopt the following principles.

## Do:

- Do make sure the team understands that feedback is a shared leadership responsibility; it is less the responsibility of King Arthur than it is of the king, knights, sage, and jester
- Do schedule routine check-in meetings
- Do keep the tone positive by encouraging team members to say what they appreciate about others' contributions

## Don't:

- Don't start the meeting with your own feedback for the team; instead, return authority to the team
- Don't shy away from performance issues; instead, address them openly as a group
- Don't get in the middle of personality conflicts; instead, facilitate difficult conversations

A useful shorthand for a leveling-up leader is CCI, or Context, Conduct, and Intent. CCI is a simple structure that you can use to deliver effective, immediate virtues-focused feedback. CCI stands for:

- **Context:** you outline the situation you're referring to, so that the context influencing behavior is clear and specific.
- **Conduct:** you discuss the person's conduct, which through one's behavior reflects adherence to virtues, and impacts team and performance.

- **Intent:** finally, you ask what his intent was behind his conduct, to highlight why he acted the way he did.

And finally, the relational dynamic being encouraged here is not about friendship as much as team performance. Everyone gathered at King Arthur's table was there, not for feasts and tournaments, but for the high-minded purpose of locating the Holy Grail. The metaphor once more applies. The best way to build relationships with your employees is to improve how you work together, not to take a break from working to engage in social activities.

## Micromanagement

If a leader routinely finds that his team levels down, a likely cause is an organizational climate or team dynamic governed by micromanagement. Signs of a classic micromanager include:

- You're never quite satisfied with deliverables
- You often feel frustrated because you would've gone about the task differently
- You laser in on the details and take great pride and pain in making corrections
- You constantly want to know where all your team members are and what they're working on
- You ask for frequent updates on where things stand
- You prefer to be cc'd on all emails

Many of us have been subject to this kind of management style. Indeed, it is so ubiquitous that micromanaging is often the default in organizations. But while one can acknowledge that there are times when careful close monitoring and careful follow-up is needed in an extreme crisis, in general micromanagement does not serve well as a long-term leadership style. It breeds distrust and creates a barrier to meaningful communication and feedback. It is either a sign of the leader's insecurity or a lack of leadership development. The results of micromanagement are a decrease in team cohesion and general apathy. The result is a team leveling down.

Executive coach Muriel Wilkins provides four suggestions if you want to stop micromanaging:

1. **Get over yourself.** There are always rationalizations for this kind of behavior, but the negative consequences are generally far greater than your stated reasons.
2. **Let it go.** The difference in management and micromanagement is in the level of detail. Avoid the minutia.
3. **Give the "what," not the "how."** There is nothing wrong with high expectations about deliverables. The difference is not dictating how to get that result. Articulate the vision, not the means of getting there.
4. **Expect to win.** The underlying psychological factor revealed in micromanaging is a fear of failure. Unresolved, however, this fear *leads* to failure. Empower your team and expect excellent results.[8]

Team leadership demands effective two-way communication. Encouraging feedback and minimizing micromanaging are essential to fostering a good organizational climate. Feedback is a catalyst for healthy teams, while micromanagement produces a toxic and dysfunctional atmosphere for team performance. A team requires a certain kind of leader, and a leader requires a certain kind of team. Both need each other for mutual leveling up. In an environment where open, honest communication is celebrated and high standards expected, where diversity is fostered by constructive feedback and trusting delegation, the teams become the sum of their combined advantages rather than any individual's particular disadvantage. It is only a team leveling up that can achieve more than the sum of its individual parts.

# CHAPTER 9

---

# COMPONENTS OF HIGH PERFORMANCE

*Where is the spiritual value of rowing? The losing of self entirely to the cooperative effort of the crew as a whole.*
— GEORGE POCOCK[1]

What George Pocock observed about the spiritual value of rowing applies to virtuous leadership. It involves a leader and teammates losing themselves entirely to the cooperative effort of the team as a whole.

Organizations are complex, and dysfunction within them is common. Typically, these dysfunctions are approached as separate problems to be solved: a lack of skilled labor, high employee turnover, a disengaged workforce, unethical behavior, and so on. However, one cannot solve the problems of an organization by focusing on each separate component. Instead, one must take a holistic systems-based approach to organizational performance. To improve the wine, you do not focus on the grape. You focus on the *terroir*. Terroir is a French term used in winemaking to describe the complete natural environment in which a particular wine is produced, including factors such as the soil, topography, and climate. Vintners know that it is the interactive dynamic, or ecosystem, that creates a distinct wine. The same is true of high performance in a team. When every member experiences losing themselves to the cooperative effort of the team, swing is achieved.

Swing is an interactive dynamic of key organizational elements and not the perfection of one single thing.

In the early 1990s I served as the site vice president of the Braidwood Nuclear Generating Station located south of Joliet, Illinois. It was a two-unit, 1250-megawatt pressurized water reactor plant and when I arrived it was regarded as one of the best electric-generating plants in the country. It was also facing challenges, competition, and internal dissent. This was at a time when more and more nuclear plants in the United States were becoming more efficient. One metric was increasingly important: outage periods. Outages are a scheduled time planned for maintenance and reactor refueling. Today, these average between 20 and 25 days. In 1992, Braidwood's outage ranged between 60 and 65 days. Our performance goal was to bring that closer to forty days. My team at Braidwood did not believe it possible.

A reason was that the owner of Braidwood, Commonwealth Edison in Chicago, was going through a difficult period with its labor unions. Every issue was contentious, especially wages and work rules. If our outage performance was to improve, it would require changes in work processes, scheduling, work rules, and would depend on the support and trust of Braidwood's unions.

The goal set was a 39-day outage. We required group managers to work alongside union personnel. Together they developed new cross-functional maintenance teams and work practices. I gained the approval of an influential union president, and two union stewards were added to my management team with full voting rights.

I, too, needed to do some work, and to help me achieve it someone followed me every day, to every meeting, discussion, and conversation, just watching and taking notes. At the end of the day, back in my office, he asked questions. "What did you hear?" "Why did you do this?" "How would you rate the meeting?" I was made to see myself in a new light, and that allowed me to gain a new perspective on my team and my own performance.

We were building what I later would term "a Company of One." We all changed, and the effort left a permanent stamp on my life. No, not every difference between workers and management was ironed out. Moments of swing were achieved among some teams, not all, and on some days, not all. But trust was forged, collective change achieved, and Braidwood became one of the first plants of its size to accomplish a 40-day planned outage in the United States.

There are three key elements to swing that must be synchronized into a harmonious whole in real time under the extreme pressure of competition. In rowing, it is often described as a ballet of pain. We have spoken of the preparatory attitudes needed for swing and the attributes necessary for it to emerge. It is now time to discuss the key elements that must be harmonized in practice. How does one pull it all together? How does one make poetry out of the various parts? Swing is elusive, but it's achievable for any crew. In the end, swing is not about winning, but rather about achieving the maximum potential from a team under stress with consistency. It is about achieving a collective harmony forged when individuals, despite reaching mental and physical breaking points, sacrifice to the cooperative effort.

The three elements that must be harmonized for swing are: leadership, technical competence, and organizational expertise. Let's look at each element more closely.

Leadership makes or breaks an organization. An organization can succeed because of a leader, but not despite a leader. This is because a leader embodies technical competence and organizational expertise and at the same time empowers the same within the organization. Absent a leader, the natural entropy of an organization left on its own sets in, driving it toward fragmentation and failure. A leader is the "cork in the bottle" when it comes to organizational performance—either blocking its potential or letting it flow. The decision to embrace qualities that release a team's resourcefulness always begins with the leader. But while leadership is necessary, it is not sufficient to achieve swing. Swing and harmonized performance always require the successful example and input of virtuous leaders, or leaders whose character, conduct, humility, selfless courage, and commitment to serve others above self is resolute.

The second key element of organizational performance is technical competence. It is having the appropriate level of knowledge, technical proficiency, skill, experience, and training for one's profession or one's team assignment. This element is given the most attention within an organization and is perhaps the easiest to identify and fix. A teacher must have subject matter mastery and the ability to connect with her students. Of the two components of a great teacher, mastery is much easier to achieve than connection. The adage attributed to

Theodore Roosevelt, "They don't care how much you know until they know how much you care," bears this out in classroom after classroom, and in team after team. This points to the third element.

The third key element is organizational expertise. It is having both an understanding of organizational dynamics as well as the virtue intelligence to release and encourage the best from the organization's people. Attitudes and conduct associated with this element include:

- Focusing on building a team
- Understanding that behavior speaks louder than words
- Establishing standards of excellence and holding people accountable to these standards
- Clearly communicating and reinforcing purpose and mission
- Developing the organization's identity and distinctiveness
- Establishing healthy relationships throughout the organization
- Building the capacity of skills and abilities of every person
- Encouraging collaborative teamwork
- Listening before acting when and where needed
- Creating an environment in which receiving and giving constructive feedback and expressing appreciation is a routine part of organizational life

When a leader can inspire people and mold them into a team, every team member develops trust. When this occurs, the team has set the conditions for further development and success. Trust engenders confidence, commitment, and a *esprit de corps* that is unbeatable.

Leadership, Technical Competence, and Organizational Expertise are the three key elements of organizational performance. More important than knowing what they are, is knowing how they interact within an organization. There are four possible interactions between a leader's technical competence (TC) and organizational expertise (OE). How these are balanced determine whether an organization fails, attains only limited capability, attains capability but at a cost, or is set up for sustained excellence.[2]

**The Leader**

| Technical Competence | Capability but at a cost | E*<br>Capability for sustained *Excellence* |
|---|---|---|
| | Failure | Limited Capability |

**Organizational Expertise**

## Failure (low TC/low OE)

Failure is guaranteed when the leader does not have the core competency to set the vision, tone, and ethos for the organization. The organization does not have the trust, behaviors, or capabilities to succeed. Without conscious and continual input from leaders, the natural entropy of an organization will always have it move in the direction of failure.

## Limited Capacity to Succeed (low TC/high OE)

A leader with a high level of organizational expertise cannot overcome his lack of technical competence. If a leader has low TC, he will have a troublesome time building trust and confidence with his followers. If the organization is low in TC, performance will suffer until the leader can identify and fill the gaps with proper training to raise TC.

A high level of organizational expertise can help develop technical competence in team members, depending on how quickly the problem is addressed. However, often it is "too little, too late" to be successful. Since organizations don't normally have the luxury of taking time off for training, it has to take place alongside assigned tasks, which can be like building a plane while it is in the air. Too frequently this means the organization finds itself too far behind the developmental curve. Sometimes management will put a new leadership team in place to address the problems, but not give them the time or space to address them. This sets up the new leadership for failure.

## High Capability But at a Relational Cost (high TC/low OE)

This organization's performance is often the most difficult to diagnose. It is viewed as good, perhaps even excellent on paper, but has uneven results. When technical competence is high and organizational expertise is low, leadership tends to "drive" the organization through micromanagement and centralized control with little regard or appreciation for their people. All too often, team members in this situation are viewed as secondary to the mission. The mantra, "Get the job done, whatever the cost," reverberates. This is sometimes referred to as a "mercenary organization." And it is death to any potential of the organization achieving swing. The mercenary at-whatever-cost ethos is a direct challenge to the virtue of relationships.

It is also costly: the visible technical competence masks the absence of relational connectivity. People are shredded. They become discouraged, disengaged, and do only what is necessary. Constructive feedback between the leader and his team is rare; lost are opportunities for a team to highlight potential problems, offer alternative solutions or suggest needed improvements. Because the problems are often more personal and subjective, they fester without being addressed. The results:

- Fluctuating performance
- Minimal organizational resiliency
- Lack of trust
- Costly and inefficient work and programs
- Leader's lack of compassion engraved into the fabric of the organization
- Low morale and retention rates, work is no longer fun, and
- Loss of talented people

Leadership is about people. When leaders ignore this, they ignore it at their own risk, as well as at the risk to their people and mission.

## E* or Sustained Excellence (high TC/high OE)

This organization has the capability for sustained excellence across the board. Though its teams' performances will have normal fluctuations, the teams can right themselves and learn from their experiences. They have resilience in both times of success and failure. In racing, no crew is going to win every race. The story of the United States 1936 crew team winning a gold medal was a three-year journey. Even when the team became very good and won the West Coast championships, they lost in the national finals. It was only after this loss, and maybe because of it, did they rebound to win the Olympic gold medal.

The leader of an E* team has developed solid technical competence and organizational expertise within herself, as well as those within her organization. She is authentic, knows her strengths and weaknesses, and recognizes that "excellence" begins with her own conduct.

There are high levels of trust throughout the organization. Everyone knows their role and responsibilities. They feel accountable for their actions, responsible to each other, and are focused on mission success, organizational improvement, and personal growth. The team is fully engaged.

The winning edge every winning shell has over its competition is the same for every winning organization—the people in the boat. People want to make a difference. People want to be fully engaged in their work. People long to experience an E* team. They want leaders of character who strive for excellence, who desire to serve and inspire and show the way. George Pocock made this point long ago, "There are no fast boats: only fast crews."[3] It is always the people who make the difference.

Excellence is not a synonym for perfection or success. Rather excellence is:

- An innate and unrelenting passion within a person or an organization to continually
  - pursue improvement, always building upon yesterday's achievements
  - build personal relationships and organizational mastery
  - admit and learn from mistakes
  - seek better practices and processes
  - develop integrated and cohesive teamwork and support
  - set high standards, and hold people accountable to these standards
  - not be satisfied with today's performance or results
  - learn from both success and failure
- About the sustained pursuit of a worthy goal, a mission, a purpose
- A lifelong journey of learning and growing

Excellence is about more than just winning a particular race. Organizations with a sustained pursuit of excellence have an engaged and highly motivated workforce, high levels of trust, well-integrated teams, better bottom lines, and better outcomes economically, socially, environmentally, and spiritually. Succinctly, the journey of excellence leads to sustained, exemplary levels of performance.

Make no mistake about it, the development of an E*

organization is extremely challenging and often entails messy work. It takes time and dedication. Yet this is the task and responsibility of every virtuous leader. Being part of an E* organization is about achieving sustained excellence and experiencing the satisfaction that you have made the difference on a team making a difference. Pocock summarizes, "When you get the rhythm in an eight, it's pure pleasure to be in it. It's easy work when the rhythm comes—that 'swing' as they call it. I've heard men shriek out with delight when the swing came in an eight; it's a thing they'll never forget as long as they live."[4]

## CHAPTER 10

---

# VIRTUE
# INTELLIGENCE
# IN PRACTICE

*When the best leader's work is done, the people say, "We did it ourselves."*

— **LAO TZU**[1]

John A. Byrne is the founder and editor-in-chief of C-Change Media. He writes, "Success will belong to companies that are leaderless—or to be more precise, companies whose leadership is so widely shared that they resemble beehives, ant colonies, or schools of fish."[2] When this is achieved, the face of the organization is the organization itself. The leader holds his organization and people accountable to the process and results, but without necessarily inserting himself into the action.

A leaderless organization is one that will fully tap into and improve its technical competence, fully realize and exceed its performance metrics, and position itself to succeed not for a single quarter or fiscal year, not for a one-and-done performance goal, but for excellence, difference-making, and collective improvement over the long haul.

Embraced, the virtue proposition allows for just such a leaderless organization. This is because in such organizations, in the end, it is not about the leader but the team. Or more precisely, it is about the leader in service to the team. Leadership begins with you, but it is not about you.

For many, this is contrarian enough to seem bizarre. We tend to limit discussions of leadership to the leader, their individual qualities, their inspiring biographies, their accomplishments. Make performance, change-making, and swing your purpose, however, and we end up focusing on the team or organization. Similarly, when we talk about emotional intelligence, too often our thinking is limited to the psychological characteristics of an individual. In fact, where emotional intelligence has the most impact is when it becomes the general ethos of the team. A premise of team leadership is that the public face of the leader is eventually subsumed by the self-leadership of the team. When this occurs, the mission, virtues, self-governance, and EQ behavior are owned by the team, the organization, the community. When this occurs, the leader and team demonstrate virtue intelligence through their conduct and performance excellence.

There is an apparent irony here. Great teams need both an external leader, for accountability and team member development, as well as an internal leader, for cohesive direction. These traits can be found in a single leader or undertaken by more than one. Regardless, the organization's leaders understand their task as developing teams and team members. They teach, help, and accompany the team as it improves, and they instill the dynamic and discipline that keeps the group from the entropy of fragmentation. And yet when success is achieved, the best teams say, confidently and without irony, "We did it ourselves."

The effective work of a leader is catalytic. In chemistry, a catalyst increases the rate of a chemical reaction without changing itself. In teams, a catalytic leader increases performance regardless of whether she changes or not, because it is not about her, but about the team. Effective teams need leadership, but only the kind of catalytic leader who returns authority to the group and empowers them to take ownership of the organization's mission, virtues, and emotional intelligence, and thereafter holds them accountable to both the process and results. An organization that calls significant attention to the leader is not an organization that is simultaneously calling attention to the importance of the team as a team.[3]

Listen to how a winning quarterback talks about the game in the post-game press conference. He couldn't have done it alone. The team went out onto the field and, as a team, did what needed to get done. Every teammate, defensive and offensive, from special teams to coaching staff, contributed, and did their part. For winning quarterbacks, speaking this way has the benefit of being true. One way to describe such a QB is as a person with high emotional intelligence. The QB's behavior at a conference tells us something about his EQ, his conduct on and off the field tells us something about his VQ. To better appreciate the difference, we need to dive deeper into understanding emotional intelligence.

There are many models and tools in the field of Emotional Intelligence. The most popular and most-often referenced of these is the EQ-i2.0 published by Multi-Health Systems (MHS) out of Toronto, Canada. The EQ-i2.0 model of Emotional Intelligence is comprised of fifteen core behaviors that can be understood, engaged, and even measured on both the individual and group levels. A leader can be Assertive, but so can an organization. An individual can be Optimistic, but so can a team. Becoming comfortable and conversant with the EQ-i2.0 model is a practical, applicable skill that improves leaders and team members. It is also essential to assessing the virtuous leader's journey, a way of understanding how far you have traveled towards virtue intelligence. What follows are summaries of each of the fifteen EQ-i2.0 behaviors and what each looks and sounds like, both when developed and when overlooked, in teams and organizations.

### Self-Regard: *Confidence in the Team*

Self-regard is the team's ability, with full recognition of its strengths and weaknesses, to both like and have confidence in itself. Self-regard is frequently used to describe NFL teams when it becomes apparent that they collectively believe in their ability to win games and overcome obstacles together. Perhaps this is most apparent when the team's players' personal lives and public lives blend together—when one's individual identity is framed increasingly as a team identity. This involves wearing the team colors as a personal fashion statement, but also as something far more profound. Teams with strong self-regard visibly put in the extra effort, go the extra mile, knowing that each of their teammates is doing the same and all for a common bigger purpose. What is interesting to note here is that personal concerns are valued and not discounted. It is only in this manner that the individual's dreams can merge with that of the team.

*Organizations that value self-regard*
- Act with pride and self-confidence
- "I" statements about accomplishments abound
- Achievements are noticed, discussed, praised, and on display
- Evidence of people's personal lives and passions are on display

*Organizations that overlook self-regard*
- Mistake self-confidence and pride for arrogance
- "I" statements are discouraged
- People wanting acknowledgement is regarded as selfish or a sign of insecurity
- Personal issues are seen as distracting

## Self-Actualization: *Commitment to Growth*

Self-actualization refers to a team's ability to grow and strive—to see potential, set meaningful goals, and work toward the betterment and fulfillment of the team. Self-actualizing teams with high EQ collectively embrace the goal of becoming better and achieving the next goal together. Some describe such teams as "learning organizations." What this reflects is, rather than an individual learning, every member of an organization is, together, committing to a shared goal of growth and improvement.

*Organizations that value self-actualization*
- Demonstrate ambition and drive toward goals
- Discuss progress, how to grow and advance, and what comes next
- Exert observable planning and pushing forward

*Organizations that overlook self-actualization*
- Treat the future and its challenges with complacency
- Exhibit comfort or resignation with life or work as it currently is
- Focus little time or effort on the future or growth

**Assertiveness:** *Acting on a Unified Identity*

Assertiveness relates to a team's ability to allow individual team members to get their needs, thoughts, and opinions out into the world, even when it might invite conflict. This encourages team members to have a strong sense of self, even in the face of disagreement. It simultaneously allows that a strong sense of self reflects a cohesive and united identity, but an identity that permits, even encourages, assertiveness.

An important, though often-overlooked, aspect of assertiveness is a team welcoming the contrarian voice. Many organizational roundtables lack the wise sage and the court jester, though as we've seen, Merlin and Dagonet were essential components of King Arthur's Camelot. An emotionally healthy organization celebrates contrarian views in its ongoing commitment to improvement.

*Organizations that value assertiveness*
- Expect command and control behaviors and see them as useful
- Expect and encourage critique, appropriate opposition, and disagreement
- Rewards those who speak up with praise, promotion, and power
- Value bold statements and critique as helpful, if not essential

*Organizations that overlook assertiveness*
- Discourage critique and debate
- Resist contrarian views
- Overlook or silence opposition, argument, and critique

## Independence: *Self-directed*

Independence refers to a team's ability to be self-directed, to go it alone when needed. This requires the team to surmount the ever-present pressure for individuals and organizations to follow the crowd, to avoid risk by following the status quo and the expected. A clear reflection of a team having a strong sense of cohesive identity is its ability to be innovative with confidence. Teams will not get ahead simply by doing what everyone else is doing. Success demands thinking outside the box. Note, however, that independence injects tension into collective action. Within a team, within an organization, how do you balance independence *and* cooperation? When encouraged by a virtues-based leader, a team learns the tension is beneficial when balanced with achieving a larger common purpose. Indeed, it is generally only strong, virtuous teams that can tolerate this tension. Innovation requires time and space for reflection. Team members require support if they are to innovate at the risk of failure. Consequently, values-driven organizations are not going to be innovative because space and support for fresh thinking is not provided.

*Organizations that value independence*
- Seek, expect, evaluate, and reward individual effort
- Value being competent and right
- Notice, value, and emphasize innovative contributions
- Value and respect time spent alone

*Organizations that overlook independence*
- Seem comfortable following the leader and/or believing the data offered by others
- Devalue or ignore new contributions and achievements of individuals
- Tend not to value or give time to and space for reflection
- Tend not to discuss, acknowledge, or celebrate individual achievements and contributions

**Interpersonal Relationships:** *Friendship with a Purpose*

Interpersonal relationships governed by trust and compassion are what allow a team to succeed. Organizations that place too much emphasis on missional solidarity will become mercenary, using people rather than respecting them. Organizations that balance solidarity with relational sociality create the conditions for friendships with a purpose, for swing. This sociality is not simply about team members being friends or getting along but doing so in the context of getting results that move the organization's mission forward. It is a relational emphasis that serves results. It is solidarity to a significant mission that gives one a sense of significance but sociality with one's team members that provides security. The combination of significance and security are psychologically necessary for high performance.

*Organizations that value interpersonal relationships*
- Offer and expect trust from one another
- Witness team members asking for help and support from others
- Maintain a warm and open environment so people care and share information

*Organizations that overlook interpersonal relationships*
- Promotes sharing and openness on a need-to-know basis
- Regard asking for help and giving compliments as unnecessary
- Do not regard trust as an important work necessity
- Smiling, friendly exchanges, and personal connections are infrequent

**Empathy:** *Awareness of Others*

Empathy is the team's ability to take notice of, be sensitive to, and do something about other people's needs and feelings. Creating the conditions where needs and feelings are noticed is essential, but not enough. Action must be taken to address team members' needs and feelings. The means of achieving this is, simply, listening.

Listening needs to become a high value practice at all levels of the organization.

*Organizations that value empathy*
- Routinely ask for and consider people's needs and perspectives in meetings and discussions
- Witness people asking about and listening to other people's needs, opinions, and feelings
- Spend time in meetings and discussions hearing from and understanding everyone, particularly those who are inclined to be quiet

*Organizations that overlook empathy*
- Leadership makes decisions heedless of their impact on people
- Witness people on the team not speaking to or caring for other people's needs, opinions, and feelings
- Regard energy and time spent on sensitivity, caring, and curiosity of others as inefficient and a waste of resources

## Social Responsibility: *Serve a Higher Cause*

Social responsibility is a team's ability and tendency to contribute to the welfare of a larger social system or organizational context, and to act with a consciousness that shows concern for and serves the greater common good. This trait is particularly important for younger workers, who place a high value on their work making a meaningful difference in the world. This means that the organization must be committed to a collective altruism that exceeds just winning, that is greater than increasing the bottom line. A strength of teams acting from the virtue proposition is that this commitment is there from the start.

*Organizations that value social responsibility*
- Are clearly serving something beyond self
- Emphasize and reward collective work
- Expect and respect sensitivity to others
- Respect "taking one for the team"

*Organizations that overlook social responsibility*
- Are not seen or regarded as client or customer-centric
- Lack a unifying compelling cause
- Have no direct connection to or concern for the wider community
- Struggle to get team members to think about and act for the greater good

**Problem-Solving:** *Emotions as a Tool*

EQ problem-solving involves a team's ability and tendency to solve problems that involve emotions and to use emotions as an effective problem-solving tool. This is a results-oriented effort that works with, not despite, the team's emotions. It is, in effect, using empathy as a problem-solving strategy. Paramount here is one's attitude toward conflict and disagreement.

*Organizations that value problem-solving*
- Witness people addressing disagreements and acknowledging feelings
- Foster open discussions about differing goals, ideas, and values
- Solves problems and engages conflict, seeing both as an opportunity for growth

*Organizations that overlook problem-solving*
- Avoid conflict
- Discounts the emotional side of problems and disagreements, leaving them undiscussed
- Views disagreements and conflicts as a hindrance or roadblock to mission

## Optimism: *Animating Hope*

Optimism is a team's ability and tendency to maintain a positive attitude even in the face of adversity. Optimism provides a team with hope and enables it to see the future, and its team members contributions to it, as positive. This is an important measure of a team's EQ because it is the cumulative effect of all the other variables. It is less of an end and more the inevitable fruit of the other variables combined in practice.

*Organizations that value optimism*
- Frequently express hope and a belief in the future and count on a positive outcome
- Regard bad times and setbacks as momentary disappointments, not predictors of what is to come

- Witness leadership looking to and speaking of the future as a place of growth, stability, and success both as an organization as well as for the team member

*Organizations that overlook optimism*
- Tend to regard the future as a place of stress, doubt, and disappointment
- Greet statements of positivity with skepticism or doubt
- Use setbacks or disappointments as evidence to confirm the negative

## Emotional Self-Awareness: *Permission to Feel*

Emotional self-awareness relates to one's ability and tendency to know what you are feeling and why. There are two challenges here. First is acknowledging your emotions, which is typically difficult for men and within some kinds of organizations. Second is being willing to explore why one is having these feelings. Organizations operating under a value proposition often do not prioritize the mindfulness and self-reflective space needed for collective self-awareness. Bottom-line considerations do not create the emotional safety that such vulnerability demands. Organizations embracing the virtue proposition, however, must create a space for self-reflection and the feelings that accompany self-scrutiny.

*Organizations that value emotional self-awareness*
- Recognize and acknowledge people for being aware of what they are feeling

- Take the time regularly to check in on how people are feeling
- Emotional vocabulary of the group is rich, which is evidence of vulnerability
- People understand what triggers their emotions

*Organizations that overlook emotional self-awareness*
- Seem not to care if people know what they are feeling
- People tend not to talk about feelings, and when they do it's viewed as a weakness, joke, or secondary
- People don't connect the mood of the group with the events of the moment

**Emotional Expression:** *Permission to Emote*

Emotional expression is related to emotional self-awareness, but captures the degree to which there is a willingness to share, to be vulnerable, and be transparent about one's feelings. One is a measure of awareness, the other is a measure of emotional expression.

*Organizations that value emotional expression*
- Are often open, disclosing, and emotive
- Demonstrate an array of emotions, including both excitement and anger
- Leadership is easy to read as they demonstrate their emotions
- Organization values authenticity and transparency

*Organizations that overlook emotional expression*

- Tend to be cautious and reserved in their communication and engagement
- Demonstrate a steady, flat emotional tone with no observable difference between good times and bad
- Value control and caution even at the expense of authenticity

## Reality Testing: *Objective Metrics*

Reality testing is a team's ability and tendency to assess honestly the here-and-now reality of any given moment or situation. What is really going on? Leaders and teams always experience pressure to describe a given moment or situation in terms of what they would like it to be rather than what it is. And, always, this runs headlong into the fact that one cannot get to "ought," without an honest assessment of what "is."

To assess what is happening, to better arrive at what ought to be done, requires a prudential tension between narrower quantitative metrics, say of sales or safety, and broader qualitative metrics, say of competence and efficiency. In all cases, however, evidential metrics must have precedence over emotions. This allows reality testing to deal primarily with how conflict is approached and resolved.

*Organizations that value reality testing*

- Have objective, fact-based conversations
- Take time to confirm perceptions and encourage objectivity
- Use words carefully

- Value and acknowledge people who change or moderate their moods when facts or understandings change

*Organizations that overlook reality testing*
- Evolve a volatile atmosphere
- Exhibit a level of drama where overstatement is common
- Engage in emotional reasoning—wherein people conclude that their feelings and emotional reactions prove something true, regardless of evidence

**Impulse Control:** *Constraint for the Team*

Impulse control relates to the team's ability and willingness to delay taking an action or stating something that is inappropriate or unproductive. In a team with strong impulse control, individual reactions are restrained while team members consider how what they say and do might impact the team. A team in control of itself is a team that eschews drama for the sake of drama. Critical is the everyday use of humor and teasing—allowing for one or more court jesters to flourish within a team—which can create the conditions whereby this boundary can be safely crossed. Safety also requires all the elements of EQ to be present: from trust and empathy, commitment and confidence, to metrics and common higher purpose. When some or all of these are weak or absent, impulse control can be in tension with assertiveness. When they are present, assertiveness is balanced by empathy to achieve impulse control.

*Organizations that value impulse control*
- Value a quiet, emotionally contained environment
- Seek and reward careful and thoughtful contributions
- Stress cautious and precise decision-making

*Organizations that overlook impulse control*
- Do not value, recognize, or reward verbal caution and restraint
- May be or appear reactive

**Flexibility:** *Willingness to Adjust*

Flexibility is a team's ability and tendency to adjust emotions, thoughts, and behavior to changing situations and conditions. In short, it is the team's ability to adapt. Being able to adjust as needed demands a learning, growing team that can take in new data and change its assumptions and approach. Conversely, a "by-the-book" approach is rarely in the best interest of a team's high-level performance.

*Organizations that value flexibility*
- View their world and work as quickly-changing and demand innovation for survival
- Exhibits humility in terms of past approaches
- Exhibits openness to new data and approaches
- Encourages people to ask questions with a spirit of exploration

*Organizations that overlook flexibility*
- See change as a threat

- Are rigid and arrogant
- Spend energy maintaining the status quo
- Resist change, preferring safety and efficiency to risk and innovation

**Stress Tolerance:** *Play the Long Game*

Stress tolerance relates to the team's ability to work effectively under conditions of pressure and urgency. It demands that an organization take the long view and manage the work/life balance of its people and teams. Such tolerance is not visible when we witness a team gut it out in a sprint. It becomes visible, however, when a team and organization demonstrates resilience and sustainability over the long haul.

*Organizations that value stress tolerance*
- View their mission as requiring endurance
- Encourage the development of strong stress management skills
- Witness people engaging in self-care through such activities as exercise, rest, meditation, and work/life programs
- Engage in new challenges, even scary ones

*Organizations that overlook stress tolerance*
- Allow and foster stress, anxiety, and fear
- Avoid new challenges for fear of stress
- Do not regard stress management skills as a priority

## Emotional Intelligence to Virtue Intelligence

The difference between a leader exercising emotional intelligence and a leader exercising virtue intelligence is captured in the difference between behavior and conduct. Simply put, behavior is transitory, reflects responses to context, and entails actions reflective of societal norms. Your behavior can change with the day of the week and the company you keep. Behavior very often bends to the norms of an organization. Conduct, on the other hand, is reflective of adherence to transcendent morals and virtues, such as love, integrity, truth, excellence, and relationships. As such it is constant over time and context. Conduct very often bends organizations to exhibited virtues.

As with the *leadership* priorities discussed in chapter six, when the five virtues are compared to the fifteen aspirational behaviors of EQ, the nine *organizational* priorities surprisingly emerge. When they become a regular part of an organization's culture, when they are the basis of and present in routine conduct, we can speak of a VQ team:

1. Confidence in the Team
2. Commitment to Growth
3. Acting on a United Identity
4. Can Go It Alone
5. Friendships with a Purpose
6. Awareness of Others
7. Serve a Higher Cause
8. Emotions as a Tool
9. Animating Hope

These nine variables are not a recipe, but rather a means of creating a collective ecosystem of overlapping healthy emotional characteristics. It is the collective combination of them that ultimately make the difference in performance. Remember, it is the *terroir* not the grape that matters most in an award-winning wine. An organization's goal is a VQ ethos across the entire organization, visible and felt in every aspect of its collective life together.

An individual with high VQ is not sufficient for an effective organization. Rather, these nine VQ characteristics need to be infused into the cultural expectations and routine conduct of the organization. Any honest team leader will recognize that achieving this is a daunting task. She can also recognize that it is achievable. Perfection is not what is needed in highly effective teams; rather, highly effective teams need an honest acknowledgement of what must be addressed and a consistent public plan to address those needs. A competent leader enlists input from the team when assessing how the team is doing on each of the nine VQ components, and she prioritizes a plan with team input to address the most flagrant needs.

Excellence is not found in the play but in the pilgrimage. It is over the journey that all the qualities necessary for success become visible. These include strong technical expertise, virtuous leaders and followers, and an organization willing to work to sustain a healthy VQ.

# CHAPTER 11

---

# BEST VERSION
# OF SELF

*Harmony, balance, rhythm, there you have it. That's what
life is all about.*
— GEORGE POCOCK[1]

The day after the explosion of Unit 4 at Chernobyl in 1986, Dr.
Armen Abagyan was a key person sent to Ukraine from Russia
to assist in taking charge of the plant and its recovery. His technical competence was off the charts. His qualities as a leader
were no less, and at times more important. It was my pleasure
and privilege to find in Dr. Abagyan a friend and a mentor.

I got to know him in the late 1990s and even more so between
2002 and 2004. Dr. Abygan was the Director General of the All-
Russian Scientific Research Institute in Moscow, his technical
grasp of nuclear plants was unsurpassed, and his pride in being
a Russian and Armenian was evident in everything he did. Most
importantly, he was also a man of great integrity and honor.
When, during one cold winter, he was turned to as someone

who could answer whether or not an aging nuclear plant could be kept online and thereby ensure Yerevan, Armenia, could keep homes warm and illuminated, he said yes, and then did what was necessary to make sure that promise was kept. He was someone who could be trusted, and throughout his life he mentored colleagues during difficult personal and professional times.

To say that Dr. Abygan displayed immense technical competence and leadership prowess during difficult times would be an incredible understatement. The decades he was involved in helping maintain, safeguard, and improve Russia's nuclear energy were difficult, complex, and historic. He did this with integrity and honor. In 2004, on the 50th anniversary of the first operational nuclear plant being connected to an external electrical grid, Dr. Abygan invited me to Obninsk, a former secret city outside of Moscow. I was the only American invited, not just as a guest but also to address the audience. I was honored to do so.

In ways large and small, organizations and performance goals test us, sometimes a little, sometimes profoundly. To meet those tests with excellence, to have the best possible chance at a difference-making performance, we need to be and to follow the best versions of ourselves.

The possibility of a team in swing requires the fusion of attitudes, attributes, accountability, and application. It requires a fusion of individuals, of leader and followers, bound together by cooperative effort towards a common goal. The most impressive high performance is realized by teams of individuals who, guided by virtue intelligence, aspire to become the best versions of themselves as team members.

"Every man in the boat had absolute confidence in every one of his mates," coach Al Ulbrickson said. "Why they won cannot be attributed to individuals, not even to the stroke of Don Hume. Heartfelt cooperation all spring was responsible for victory."[2]

The virtuous proposition allows and amplifies heartfelt cooperation. Virtues—love, integrity, truth, excellence, relationships—define the characters of leader and follower. It is evident in the virtue intelligence with which technical competence is demonstrated. Purpose, goals, and accountability are transparent and shared. Swing is the result, measurable in performance.

Swing does not occur in a racing shell unless there is harmony, balance, and rhythm. For this to happen, there needs to be an outside observer who is willing to spend time observing, listening, challenging, and encouraging the oarsman, individually and as a team, moving them beyond themselves to something greater, from individual achievement to team greatness. While Ulbrickson developed the rowing tangibles of the team, Pocock worked on their intangibles—their hearts. Both were needed if they were ever to reach for the stars.

Our personal lives are no different. We will never experience swing until there is a deep internal sense of harmony, balance, and rhythm. It is not something we can will into place. Blind spots, preconceived notions, and false illusions inevitably hinder our inner development. No one achieves their best potential on their own. Outside help is always needed.

Leaders need mentors. Teams need mentored leaders. The fulcrum is character. A virtuous mentor is the pivot around which a leader turns, learning that leadership begins with you, but it is not about you.

## HOLISTIC MENTORING

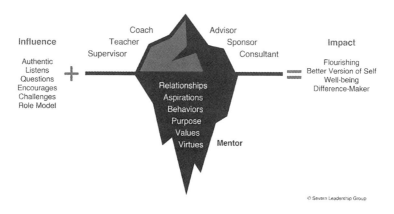

The illustration above describes what is essential for a leader to become a better version of himself. It is a version one grows into overtime and with the assistance of an outside mentor. The term *mentor* can be defined in several ways. Within *The Virtue Proposition,* I mean specifically, "holistic mentoring." In plain terms, the holistic mentoring process is defined by this template:

*Influence + Mentoring = Impact.*

## Influence

An effective mentor is first and foremost a person who has experienced harmony, balance, and rhythm in her own life. She knows who she is and who she is not. As a mentor, she brings a unique insight and perspective to the mentor-mentee relationship. She has good relational skills and can build trust by being open and honest. The role of the mentor is to listen, question, challenge, and to encourage her mentee. The mentor serves as a role model—never perfect, but also willing to learn, change, and grow herself. The holistic mentor-mentee relationship is not about meeting for six sessions and then shutting the door. The relationship is part of a life-long journey for both the mentor and mentee. The influence is mutual and reciprocal.

## Mentoring

Leadership is defined by your character and is based on a set of timeless and transcendent virtues—love, integrity, truth, excellence, in the context of relationships. The core of a leader is the totality of who you are and what you are about. This core serves as your inner compass, which is best measured under pressure. Courage, as expressed by C. S. Lewis, "is not simply one of the virtues, but the form every virtue takes at the testing point."[3] The same is true for mentors.

Leadership is a developmental process, a pilgrimage. Progress is evident in your conduct. Holistic mentors act the sage and the court jester, the coxswain and the coach during a mentee's journey.

Your invisible core is expressed by your conduct. Your character and behavior interact with each other, each influencing the other in an ongoing dynamic. Your sense of well-being, or wholeness, is realized when your conduct reflects an inner life of harmony, balance, and rhythm—the best version of yourself.

The role of the mentor is to help you achieve this balance. The mentor cannot do this for you. This is a journey of growth that must be undertaken by each leader alone with the mentor's assistance.

There are two sides to this process: what is seen and what is unseen. Like an iceberg, what is below the waterline is what is most significant. Below the surface and at a much deeper level, the mentor works with the aspiring leader to develop and demonstrate her ability to build stronger relationships, articulate aspirations, and demonstrate behaviors, purpose, and virtues over time. This is the kind of leadership formation that the Severn Leadership Group provides.

The purpose of the mentor is not to just provide advice or to play the expert, but to walk with you during the process: to help you see yourself clearly within a lived context at the testing point and to encourage you to incrementally level up to achieve the best version of yourself. Recall that the measure of a leader is his willingness to be held accountable to others, to learn to see himself accurately, to assess his conduct honestly, and to work continually to improve. To be your best you need a mentor. To achieve your best from a mentor, a leader must be open, honest, willing to change, and to be held accountable. To benefit the most from mentoring, you must be willing to answer such questions as:

1. What is your story?
2. What do see as your purpose in life or your life's goal?
3. What do you want people to say about you on your 80th birthday?
4. What energizes you? What drains you?
5. Share your strengths and weaknesses. What behaviors do you want to change?

6.  Do you have any time bombs in your life? If you were to have a fall—publicly or privately—what would be the reason?
7.  Who is the most influential person in your life? How would you rate your friendships?
8.  What keeps you up at night?
9.  Do you sense you are well-suited for your current work?
10. Were you raised in a family with a particular worldview? A spiritual or religious tradition?
11. What are you most afraid of?

## Impact

Once you have experienced the power of harmony, balance, and rhythm, you will never forget it. The first time is transformative. The power of the 1936 gold medal-winning crew is its proof of concept: there, for everyone to see, is the result of a team in harmony, balance, rhythm, a team in swing.

Leaders recognize that they need to be mentored because they know that the team members over which they have responsibility will need the same. We cannot be an influence on others unless we are first willing to be influenced by others. The measure of a leader is his or her willingness to be a follower first. The emerging leader will need to learn how to be mentored as well as to subsequently mentor others. It is a means by which the leader pays it forward to the next generation.

Developing the best team begins with the leader being the best team member. This is a process achieved over time, through a willingness to be vulnerable, by listening to others, encouraging them, and taking the integration and development of virtues and relationships seriously. In short, swing in a team begins with finding swing in your life.

The rewards are lifelong. Of all the ways you spend your time, being mentored in your leadership has one of the highest returns on investment. The late Clayton Christensen was a distinguished Harvard Business School professor and author of *How Will You Measure Your Life?* He writes, "The only metrics that will truly matter to my life are the individuals whom I have been able to help, one by one, to become better people."[4]

It is within the relationship of mentor and mentee, mutually aiding the other on a pilgrimage of leadership, that the calling to be a change-maker is met.

High performance leadership begins with the attitude in the leader that development is needed and possible. This sets her on this journey. The aim is to embody the attributes of transcendent virtues. This is accomplished with the accountability of a mentor who assesses the emotional intelligence *and* the virtue intelligence of the leader and the team and incrementally begins the process of establishing trust, affection, and shared commitment to growth and mutuality.

The essence of leadership is the leader-follower dynamic observed and aided by a mentor. When a team is more than one individual, it is the relational dynamic between the leader and each team member as well as between each team member that matters. Each person brings a unique combination of experience, knowledge, skills, abilities, and personality to the team. Fusing these into a seamless whole is the task of the leader and the ultimate measure of a team. High performance is the consequence, but not the aim. The aim is this fusion. The individuals must be first turned into a team.

The burden of this book is to make the case that this process is essential, is often overlooked, and requires a different kind of leader than is usually celebrated. The ultimate measure of a high performing team leader is his or her ability to foster this fusion of individuals.

Because there is no one-size-fits-all recipe for this, because every individual is different and every collection of individuals is different, the relational dynamic between the leader and follower is paramount for success. This demands that a leader be able to know her own strengths and weaknesses. Be able to assess the same in each team member and work incrementally toward a collective attunement of passion and purpose. It requires that the leader actively return authority to the team, empower them in their technical skills and relational competence, and then get out of the way, effecting a kind of invisible enabling.

This is what we see enacted in the 1936 Olympic gold medal race. The coach's directive that Don Hume was too sick to race was challenged by the team. The coach listened to the team and got out of the way. In this way, they were collectively empowered to face the inevitable obstacles that the race brought to them. It was their race. The coach was not in the boat and could at that point have no direct influence on the results.[5] But by creating the long-sustained dynamics between the oarsmen over the course of the previous months together, they were able to rally for a come-from-behind victory over two powerful state-sponsored crews from Germany and Italy. By the time the race arrived, Pocock as mentor to Ulbrickson, Ulbrickson as mentor to coxswain and crew, and each crew member's mentoring of each other, including the ill Hume, has been subsumed by the team, its purpose, its unquestioned common commitment, and its determination to succeed.

The lasting point here is that there are two senses of swing. There is the technical swing in the rowing of the boat when perfect harmony is achieved in the fusion of each stroke. But even more important, and more difficult to achieve, is the fusion of the relational dynamics of trust and inspiration between the oarsmen. *In the end, it is establishing the relational conditions for swing that must be the aim of all team leaders.* It is in these conditions that the combined dynamics of virtue, character, humility, vulnerability, and trust are put to the test in the crucible of individual pain and collective competition. This is the "heartfelt cooperation" of which Al Ulbrickson spoke. This is the measure of leaders of high performance teams. The virtue proposition is finally in service to creating the conditions for swing within a team or organization.

# CHAPTER 12

---

# SIGNS OF A HEALTHY ORGANIZATION

When my daughter was eight she taught me an invaluable leadership lesson. We were in the living room. I was absorbed in a newspaper while she chatted away. She stopped to ask, "Dad, are you listening to me?"

"I am," was my reply.

She continued to talk, only to again stop and ask. "Daaad, are you listening?" I gave her the same reply. A few minutes later, the same question, my same answer, except this time Kristen tore the paper from my hands.

"Okay," she said. "Dad, what did I just say?"

I hadn't a clue because I hadn't, in fact, been listening. And now that she had my undivided attention, she was direct. "You are not listening to me! I want to talk to you!"

This is not just a homely anecdote plucked from my personal life. It goes immediately to the application of the virtue proposition as a practice and a habit. If you say you're listening, then listen, and this applies in your living room *and* your office. Like gravity, like character, the application of the virtue proposition applies equally everywhere, including in my own home. My daughter made that quite clear. When you start to look, when you seek out the gravitational pull of virtues, you will discover its effects the world over.

The virtue proposition captured on film is the picture of the gold medal ceremony at the 1936 Olympics. In it, you see coxswain Bobby Moch standing on the top of the podium with the other oarsmen trailing behind him on the ground.[1] Moch, as coxswain, was the smallest of the athletes in the winning Olympic U.S. rowing eight. He never pulled an oar. Yet he was the unquestioned leader of the winning boat and took his place atop the medal stand. Even more than their coach, he was the person the oarsmen depended on and it was Moch's commands they followed in the heat of the battle. This was so much the case that Moch and his oarsman had developed their own secret language. "SOS" for "slow on slides," and "WTA" for "wax their ass," and "BS" for "beat the sophs."[2]

The precise meanings matter less than the fact that their cohesion was so complete, their focus on the common outcome so understood, that shorthand was all they needed to speak and be heard.

An Olympic eight is an organization in microcosm. They are healthy when their culture, purpose, strategy, leadership, and followership fit together in an inclusive and consistent way. Are people engaged in their work or merely putting in their time? Do people trust each other? Is there a sense of purpose and enduring standard of excellence? Do they feel they are valued and are making a difference?

The personal dynamic Moch established with the oarsmen ultimately made all the difference. It is not surprising that he would later become the head crew coach at Massachusetts Institute of Technology, that he would earn a law degree from Harvard Law School and win a case in front of the U.S. Supreme Court. He was a leader.[3]

The leader sets the tone for the crew, the team, the organization. On one hand, an authentic, virtuous leader inspires, encourages, and develops each member of the team and, in doing so, betters the team. The standards and expectations are high despite the challenges or circumstances facing the team. The members of a well-led team, however, know their backs are covered. They will have all the necessary support and will not be hung out to dry if something does not go as planned. Every person counts and is counted on.

But a leader can also be toxic. The telltale signs are common. The team's mission is vague. Roles and responsibilities are not clearly defined. There is little communication in the form of helpful feedback. As micromanagement replaces leadership, team members come to think of their work as nothing more than as tasks to complete in fulfillment of their jobs. The toxic manager will eventually extinguish the life and potential of the team.

Critical in a healthy organization is the dynamic of the relationships forged around the pursuit of a common purpose.

Some leaders mistake the relational aspect of leadership as suggesting that they engage their followers with small talk. Team members, however, are not expecting this of leaders. It doesn't matter to them if you talk about sports, politics, TV shows, or the weather. None of these touch on why they are there, what they are there to accomplish. Team members want to engage the leader in work-related conversations that enable them to grow professionally. Bestselling author Kim Scott writes, "The best way to build relationships with your team is to improve how you work together, not to take a break from working."[4]

This demands the use of constructive feedback. It involves discussions about personal performance, strengths, project performance, areas for growth—where things went well and areas that need to be improved—and overall team performance. The leader also needs to be open to feedback from the rest of the team. Where does he need to improve? How can she better support the team? Where is there a need for more resources?

Feedback is shorthand for structured listening, which is the foundational building block of team relationships. Open communication helps to improve overall performance. It is how issues are identified and resolved before they become problems. When individual and team performance is reviewed, people have an opportunity to reflect on their work, make changes, and revise plans that ultimately result in improved performance and personal satisfaction.

It is important for the discussions to be honest, frank, and specific. The high performing leader gets to know her people on a deeper level through open communication focused on their collective ambitions. How can we improve? What's lurking around the corner? When people feel like they are being heard and have the means to be heard, seeds of trust are planted. Teams are not simply built on the practice field or in competition, but in the ongoing process of structured feedback.

Jamie Dimon, Chairman and CEO of J.P. Morgan Chase & Co., cautions his people that one of the major derailers of performance is when an organization forgets its A-B-Cs. These three must be avoided at all costs.

**A** – Arrogance      **B** – Bureaucracy      **C** – Complacency

Any or all of the A-B-Cs erode an organization's ability to learn, innovate, and grow. They are organizational killers. You must learn to recognize and eliminate them.[5]

Organizational psychologist Roger Schwartz writes, "When a team works well together, it's because its members are operating from the same mindset and are clear about their goals and their norms."[6] Everyone is on the same page as to how they are going to be held accountable.

Giving and receiving feedback is a skill. Few people are naturally good at it. Developing this skill is obviously critical to fostering relational swing. Schwartz adds that the old management mantra, "Praise in public, criticize in private," is inappropriate in team settings. When teams have problems, it should all be out in the open so that ownership of the problem is team-wide. Harmony when achieved despite conflict avoidance and ineffective feedback routines is a pseudo-harmony that will not lead to high performance.

A healthy organization breeds high performance, determined by its ability to deliver over a prolonged period meaningful, measurable, and financially sustainable results for the people or causes the organization is in existence to serve. But to identify a healthy organization, noting its performance isn't enough. Similarly, though a high performing team depends on its leader, you can most quickly identify a healthy organization by the qualities it displays:

- Clarity of purpose
- An engaged workforce
- High morale
- High retention rates
- Clear communication
- Constructive feedback, particularly when self-critical
- Openness to learning and
- Objective metrics

The same holds true for a dysfunctional organization. They can sometimes produce results, though rarely sustained results. And they can sometimes have a charismatic leader. But signs of organizational dysfunction are visible in the use of micromanagement.

There are times when detailed follow-up may be needed, but micromanagement does not serve well as a long-term leadership style. Over time this style of leadership breeds mistrust and discontentment. It is either a sign of the leader's insecurity or the lack of effective employee development. Micromanagement destroys team cohesion.

Teams are built by listening to each other honestly through constructive two-way feedback. Feedback is a catalyst for healthy teams, while micromanagement produces toxic and a dysfunctional atmosphere for team performance. Relational swing can only occur when a leader models and manages these strategic dynamics between himself and the team and between the other team members. Such dynamics do not happen without the example and initiative of the leader. For a team to become a team, the leader must lead, even when this leadership is not about the leader. This is as true in an organization as it is in an Olympic eight rowing shell. The oarsmen wait on the coxswain's voice.

When constructed along the axis of purpose and change-makers, the most potent team leadership eclipses team and organization and causes a shift in the wider world. This happens when a healthy organization forges a dense network.

For years, no one took University of Washington rowing and its blue-collar lumberjack oarsmen seriously. Not until they won the 1936 Berlin Olympics. From there, the teamwork taught, demonstrated, and experienced in the University of Washington rowing program created a dense network of highly successful rowing coaches.

Gordon Newell writes:

> Those Washington crews of the 1920s and 1930s provided an amazing number of outstanding coaches to universities all across America. Bob Moch distinguished himself as Washington freshman coach, and varsity coach at MIT. Harrison Sanford coached Cornell's 'Big Red' crew for many years. . . . Among the other Washington oarsmen who, after graduation, did their turns as coaches with great distinction were Brad Raney–Columbia, Gus Erickson–Syracuse, Loren Schoel–Marietta, Jim McMillin–MIT, Vic Michaelson–Brown, Charles Logg–Rutgers, Gene Melder–Clark, Mike Murphy–Wisconsin, Dutch Schoch–Princeton, and Ellis MacDonald–Marietta.[7]

George Pocock and Al Ulbrickson created an enduring legacy throughout the U.S. collegiate rowing community through these other coaches. It was not only Pocock's wooden shells that prevailed, but Pocock's rowing philosophy of teamwork that established a far larger community of success. When, in 1956, George Pocock was the recipient of the Rowing Citation Award for outstanding contributions to the sport of rowing, his citation called him "probably the best-loved man in the sport of rowing."[8] Paralleling the breadth of his influence was the depth of his modesty. He is paradigmatic of a catalytic leader of a dense network.

The social sciences are clear that the main actor on the stage of social change and influence is not the lone individual but the dense network. A person can initiate a cause, but if the cause is to make a difference, it will be because a network has been forged. A dense network is a kind of social entity that is aligned to a shared mission that is reinforced relationally that enables a cause to gain momentum and influence.[9] Pocock's influence made rowing a national collegiate sport within the United States and broadened its area of dominance from Northeastern elite universities to all the major universities on the West Coast, starting with his beloved University of Washington. Pocock's national network of influence did not begin at Harvard on the Charles River, but in Washington state on Lake Washington.

More importantly, Pocock's dense network arose to meet a larger purpose to which he dedicated his life. George Pocock grew up in England from a long line of rivermen. Here, rowing was not a sport but a way of life, an everyday form of transportation on the Thames River. After immigrating to the Pacific Northwest, he devoted his life to the craft of making wooden boats. Over the course of his life, George was offered the head coaching job at numerous universities, all of which he refused. He knew that American rowing badly needed shells, and that if he signed up with one university, American rowing would suffer. His cause was making rowing as influential a collegiate sport in America as it was in England. Through his own personal sacrifices, exemplar of character, excellence in craftmanship, and investment in the lives of his oarsmen, the George Pocock dense network changed the face of U.S. rowing forever.

Dense networks are a flywheel in social change—how one makes a difference in the world. What animates dense networks are catalytic leaders. This is a leader who publicly sacrifices his own agenda for that of the team, who routinely returns authority to the team, who finds ways to empower the team without calling attention to himself while maintaining ongoing mutual accountability. When done well, the catalytic leader is increasingly replaced by a catalytic network—the team itself becomes the animating agent in the life and direction of the team, its public face. Let's unpack what this involves.

There is a common assumption that most leaders are aiming to further their own agenda, frequently through some means of coercion. This assumption must be consciously reversed if one is to be a catalytic leader in a team. The leader must demonstrate in action that their priority is the well-being and flourishing of his followers. Most often this demands doing something that involves the leader experiencing personal sacrifice. Sacrifice is the way in which a leader's authenticity is established and credibility restored. In a work environment, this might mean accepting top-down criticism, delaying a promotion, standing up for a colleague when costly, and the like. The point is that words alone are not going to suffice; only action taken on behalf of the team, even when at a personal cost, will work.

Likewise, returning authority involves far more than just delegating. It means continuously considering who is the appropriate decision-maker in each situation, who will bring ownership and pride to making sure the issue is addressed effectively. The leader must selectively cede decision-making power to her subordinates, giving them permission to fail. This does not mean that the leader abdicates responsibility for the results; the buck still stops with the senior leader. But it does mean empowering one's followers so that they carry the weight of the responsibility for their decisions and actions. This is how a leader expresses trust in and for his team.

To do this effectively, the leader must provide the resources and empowerment the team needs to succeed. Ideally, this occurs behind the scenes and does not result in attention and accolades to the leader. As the team is empowered and authority returned to it, the leader should become much less visible.

However, this growing invisibility is not an abandonment of ongoing mutual accountability. Two-way feedback remains necessary and mutual commitment to the results paramount.

The need to lead but empower followers with choice and accountability creates an ongoing tension. It is navigable by leaders with a high degree of empathy and virtue intelligence. Leadership is a necessity for a team, but only when the team's success, not the leader's personal agenda, is the recognized priority. The leader must cede authority without abdicating responsibility. The leader must become increasingly invisible as the team's prominence increases, while maintaining ongoing mutual accountability. The person capable of managing these tensions in a manner that creates trust in his team is the virtuous leader that demonstrates high performance. It is in the balancing of these conflicting motivations and behaviors that a catalytic leader emerges and a powerful dense network capable of lasting influence is created.

Aspiring leaders should not only look for a mentor, but also for a network of like-minded leaders who can collectively challenge them to be their best. Many leaders do not feel allowed, let alone encouraged to talk openly about their challenges and opportunities. When possible, leaders should join a larger network of leaders who share their passions, values, and virtues, and are collectively committed to one another.

Archimedes said that if you were to give him a fulcrum and a lever long enough, he could move the world. To meet the contemporary leadership crisis, we need a dense network of leaders capable of moving the world toward the better.

A dense network requires a catalyst, cause, community, and context. While a dense network cannot emerge at all without a leader, a dense network cannot function well without a particular kind of leader. He must be a virtuous leader, his effectiveness and character visible in his conduct. Such a leader will be able to connect relationally, curate ideas, and champion the cause. In doing so, he must truly believe that the team is paramount, and its flourishing in service to their mutual mission is his highest priority.

# CHAPTER 13

---

# CHANGE OR CHANGE

*While some boat builders try to tell you that the boat makes a difference, we know that cultures of excellence are created by athletes, coaches, and their support networks. It is the hard work and teamwork of these stakeholders that win races and create positive and transformative boathouse environments.*
- **POCOCK RACING SHELLS WEBSITE**[1]

With the war effort ramping up, collegiate rowing was in limbo. Pocock and his crew had been hired to work for The Boeing Company to make wooden pontoons for seaplanes. When General Crowder, head of the national draft, visited the Boeing shop, he watched Pocock work for a few minutes. Just days earlier, Pocock had been offered an exemption from wartime service due to missing two fingers on his right hand. Pocock, determined to serve, refused the exemption. The General said, "I see you are prepared to fight the Germans." Pocock answered, "Sir, I will be proud to go." The General replied, "You can be of far more use to the war effort right where you are."

As such, Pocock's career pivoted to making wooden Curtiss HS-2L flying boats.

Change is inevitable. It is also when excellence and difference-making are catalytic to a team or an organization, or when they are not.

As World War II came to an end, Boeing orders were cut in half. With time on their hands, Pocock's team built two racing shells in the large Boeing hanger. Ironically, it was these two racing shells that launched Boeing back into the airplane business. A congressional committee from Washington was reviewing wartime aircraft plants to determine if they were worthy of further government contracts.

There in the empty Boeing hanger lay the gleaming sixty-foot-long new shells. One member of the committee reviewed them closely. "Who on earth built these? I rowed at Harvard, and I never expected to see anything like this out here. I would like to meet the builders and talk to them." Edgar Gott, the general manager of the plant added, "That's the kind of workmen we have here." Shortly afterward, Boeing received orders for two hundred pursuit planes. Whether building racing shells or planes, Pocock's winning philosophy translated to new opportunities.[2]

What differs among organizations is how they understand and implement change. Building on the work of Edgar and Peter Schein's *The Corporate Culture Survival Guide,* John Kotter's *Leading Change,* Clayton Christensen's "The Tools of Cooperation and Change," as well as my own personal experience, we have developed the Severn Leadership Group Organizational Change Model.[3] It highlights two essentials. First, organizations must learn to adapt to change. Second, managing the inevitability of change within a team or organization places a special demand on its leaders as change often engenders fear and decreases trust.

The two axes create quadrants that are similar to the Individual Change model, which we discussed earlier. But here they help track a team or organization's path towards collective, collaborative excellence.

## Organizational Change Model

| | |
|---|---|
| **Arrogant**<br>Cyclic<br><br>*Leadership* | **Excellence**<br>E*<br><br>Continuous Improvement |
| **Adrift**<br>Unsatisfactory<br><br>*Intervention* | **Struggling**<br>Marginal<br><br>*Leadership* |

Performance (vertical axis)

**Fearless Reviews, Desire Improvement**

## Horizontal Axis

The horizontal axis of Fearless Reviews and Desire Improvement represents the degree to which an organization will look critically at its performance, people, processes, and its commitment to their purpose/mission. The most resilient organization does not fear what they will learn when performance reviews are conducted. They have an inherent desire for continuous improvement. This axis is about the organization's willingness to change and move toward excellence.

## Vertical Axis

The vertical axis is the metric of the organization's overall performance as it moves towards excellence. It is the degree to which the mission/purpose is being fulfilled. Several indicators can assess this performance, depending on the organization and its size.

### Adrift: No fearless reviews and minimum desire to improve with unsatisfactory performance

Adrift, or the bottom left quadrant, is nowhere any team wants to be. Organizations stuck here face a bleak long-term outlook. Poor morale, low standards, and unsatisfactory performance characterize this organization with little hope or desire for change. Meaningful performance metrics are not evident or used. The organization is functioning without a rudder or compass and is consequently adrift in the doldrums. An outside organizational intervention is required.

Someone must step in and create a *sense of urgency*. She must be direct and to the point. The organization must face the facts about its performance and own them. Either it changes or it will not survive. This is a tough message, but it must be communicated. For some, it will be welcome and overdue. Others would rather leave than change. Regardless, the message is simply: "Change or change"—change the way we work or change where you work.

It is important for the leader of an organization that is adrift to assemble a specific team to guide the change process. Kotter writes, "This is a powerful group—guiding the change—one with leadership skills, credibility, communication skills, authority, analytic skills, and a sense of urgency."[4] To the degree that outsiders are brought in to be a part of this team, which is often necessary, it increases the challenge of establishing the necessary dynamics of trust.

The leader guiding this change must be authentic and exhibit the alignment of her conduct to the core behaviors of love, integrity, truth, excellence, and relationships. She must be fully committed to her people and her organization. This is essential for developing healthy relationships and creating increased levels of trust. This gets the change process underway.

## Struggling: Fearless reviews and desire to improve with poor performance

An organization in the bottom right quadrant, Struggling, has the potential to recover. It wants change, but it does not know how to change. Nor does it have a clear sense of what excellence looks like. For the leader of a struggling team, a good place to begin is for him and his new team to review thoroughly performance data. Dig into the details and look for trends. Ask why performance is as it is. The results could be quite revealing for everyone.

At this point the leader must establish a well-communicated and understood goal and purpose of the team. Her next steps are to empower others to act, develop teamwork, and provide technical training where needed. Together the team must standardize policies and procedures, performance metrics, and develop a strong fearless review process. It is important for them to have some short-term wins. It may now be a good time for the team to visit with a high performing team (inside or outside the organization) to see how it is done and observe their best practices.

Leading a struggling team is difficult and often frustrating work, but there are no shortcuts. Building a new team, setting the standards and expectations, and developing a high level of trust takes time. Know that all this work will pay huge dividends in the end; it is how you begin to bend the curve out of struggling and into excellence.

## Arrogant: No fearless reviews and minimum desire to improve with high performance

The Arrogant team is perhaps the most difficult organization to tackle. Their overall performance is excellent, but it is not sustainable. Somewhere, over time, they have lost their ability to be self-reflective. Cracks in their performance go unnoticed. Complacency sets in and performance begins to either ebb or stagnate, as other organizations around them continue to improve and set new standards for performance. A downturn in performance metrics is ignored or considered momentary. Their transitory excellence breeds the delusion that they do not need to change.

There is a second version of this quadrant. It is when a forceful leader has driven the team's performance to high levels. From the outside looking in, many classify the resulting organization as a top performer. The leadership team in this case, however, is a one-man-band. When this leader departs, organizational performance drops and the rest of the organization collapses—worn out and not prepared to forge ahead on their own. In all instances, this is the result of a values-based leader for whom shorter-term performance is put above longer-term difference-making.

In the first case, the organization is arrogant in the sense that they believe, having obtained excellent performance results, their journey is complete. "We will just keep doing what we are doing today, and we will do just fine." Which is true until change is required, and, as we know, change is inevitable.

In the second case, the one-man-band is in a state of arrogance. He views himself as an effective leader. "Look at my performance!" Unfortunately, when you look at what he leaves behind, there is a trail of untapped potential, missed opportunities for team development, and collapsing performance.

A leader tasked with an arrogant team must lead by example, exhibiting in her conduct the virtues (love, integrity, truth, excellence, and relationships) day in and day out. The core of the organization needs to be restored. This begins by listening, building relationships and trust, watching, questioning, encouraging, challenging, communicating, setting clear standards, developing new teams, and restoring the organization's understanding of what is needed and what is possible. Expect resistance. Arrogant organizations are still performing well and they will question change at first. The long-term view must be encouraged over short-term thinking and metrics.

## Excellence or E*: Fearless reviews and desired improvement = excellent performance

The E* organization has the capacity for sustained excellence in the face of change and over time. Though their performance will have normal fluctuations, they are able to make improvements and learn from their experiences.

Excellent organizations exhibit a high level of trust at every level. Everyone knows their role and responsibilities. They feel accountable for their actions, and responsible for each other. They are focused on mission success, organizational improvement, and personal growth. This team is fully engaged.

The leader has developed solid technical competence and organizational expertise within herself, as well as those within her organization. She is authentic, knows her strengths and weaknesses, and recognizes that excellence begins with her own conduct and actions.

The key to staying in this quadrant is teams that are open to critical feedback both from internal and external sources and leaders and followers who never become complacent. This organization understands the difference between success and excellence. They know when to celebrate and when it is time to move on.

No two organizational change transformations are identical, but the fundamentals required by each remain the same. If we are to be leaders of change, leaders of transformation, we must understand the challenges and opportunities involved in moving a team toward organizational excellence. Leading change takes courage, commitment, and a sense of personal well-being. All of these reflect leaders grounded by transcendent virtues and animated by making a lasting difference.

An organization can change only to the degree its leadership will change. While accomplishing this, a leader's personal conduct will be clearly put to the test. Love of team and team members is demonstrated by a leader acting with courage, sacrificing her time, and giving her team her full attention. Integrity is key to seeing what is truly happening and resolving conflicts among the team. Speaking truth can motivate change and build relationships with customers and the team. Excellence can drive change and make the future attractive. Finally, relationships become even more essential in times of change; they are what unify leaders and the team, bring new partners in to support change, and attract customers in the future. Combined, these elements—love, integrity, truth, excellence, relationships—is very effective and the only way to sustain excellence.

## The Dynamics of Accepting Change

Arriving at excellence, for a team adrift, struggling, or arrogant, is neither easy or quick. This is captured by another model reflecting the requirements of a leader facilitating organizational change. It is the response curve.

This curve is adapted from a model originally developed by Elizabeth Kubler-Ross in the 1960s to explain the grieving process and accepting the inevitability of death and dying.[5] Since then, it has been used by many in one form or another as a method of helping people understand their reactions to significant change. This version of the model has four basic stages: denial, resistance, exploration, and commitment.

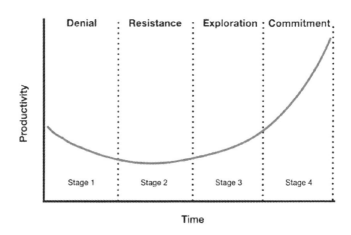

## Denial (Stage 1)

In the denial stage, the organization experiences shock. The first question is, "Why do we have to change?" Even among the struggling and the adrift, the status quo is assumed to be either just fine or good enough. People confronting change often feel threatened. People are fearful of the unknown.

A leader of a team in denial needs to anticipate:

- *What you see*: indifference, disbelief, and avoidance
- *What you hear*: silence, it will never happen, it won't affect me
- *Approach*: listen and communicate what you know and can share often

## Resistance (Stage 2)

As the shock of necessary change wears off, resistance sets in. Often the blame game begins—finding someone else or something else to blame. There is great suspicion and frustration within a team and across an organization. Morale sinks. At this point resistance bottoms out. As people accept that change is genuine, apathy or remoteness sets in.

A leader of a team in resistance needs to anticipate:

- *What you see*: anger, complaining, glorifying the past, skepticism, unwillingness to take part
- *What you hear*: "it won't work," "it used to be . . ." "the data is flawed"
- *Approach*: watch, listen, acknowledge, validate, support

## Exploration (Stage 3)

As the darker emotions of Stage 2 subside, a more optimistic vantage point emerges. People accept the fact that change is inevitable. They think about: new opportunities, new goals, necessary training, how best to be organized. A leader must encourage this exploration to be about the organization rather than the individual, who may take this moment as an opportunity to look for new work elsewhere. This stage raises many questions among team members and the need for thoughtful answers from its leaders. Hope and trust are on the rise, but are also being tested.

A leader of a team in exploration must anticipate:

- *What you see*: energy, risk averesion, impatience, activity without focus
- *What you hear*: optimism, I have an idea, let's try, what if?
- *Approach*: give time to explore and test, develop capability, celebrate small wins

## Commitment (Stage 4)

Exploration turns to commitment. Development plans are made. Additional responsibilities and specific tasks are put into place. There is a greater sense of energy and enthusiasm. People want to move on and get the change behind them. Organizational loyalty increases.

A leader of a team embracing commitment can expect:

- *What you see:* future orientation, initiative, confidence
- *What you hear:* how can I contribute, let's get on with it
- *Approach*: celebrate and commend

This response-curve model is useful for both individuals and groups. The speed that they move through each stage varies. Some will do so faster than others. Often, this is a reflection of the qualities of the leaders within an organization. If people do not feel adequately heard and supported, then they may get stuck, or even move backward.

Leaders must appreciate the processes by which change happens and understand what state the organization is in. This means that anticipated change must be carefully planned and communicated at every level. Rarely does ramming a change through work. The need for change may be very clear, but individuals and organizations need to feel appreciated and supported throughout all the inevitable stages and steps that change requires. Sensitivity to the process is key.

The winds of change are never going away. This is truer today than ever before; the pace of disruption is increasing. The average worker is expected to change their careers twelve times over the course of their lives. Organizations that have long been resistant to change are the very ones most likely to experience the most abrupt and cataclysmic change. The question of how one leads an organization through change has become increasingly important. There is no magic process or guarantee of success. But the inevitability of change establishes the environment in which both leaders and followers will be most tested. The difference-makers in this situation are:

- A diverse group of men and women;
- Who live with a strong sense of purpose
- Who exhibit strong character, conduct anchored by a set of timeless and transcendent virtues
- Who appreciate that life is ultimately about relationships and people
- Who leverage today's challenges for a flourishing tomorrow
- Who listen, learn, and act
- Who know they need others and create a team
- Who are people of courage and hope
- Who live consciously between what is and what can be, and
- Who are authentic

When Pocock pivoted his career from building rowing shells to airplane pontoons, he could blame the war effort for the inevitability. But it was his acceptance of the change, reestablishing his team at Boeing, and maintenance of high standards that set his leadership apart. We tend to tell the stories of great men as random snapshots rather than as moving pictures. Doing so misses the importance of unchanging transcendent virtues in navigating change. Pocock was eventually able to return to his first love of building rowing shells and establish the company Pocock Racing Shells. Decades later, the emphasis on excellence in teamwork and network is evidenced in the company. The power of team still stands out. This chapter opens with the principle of team-based achievement that anchors Pocock's company. It goes on to affirm:

> When you bring a Pocock Racing Shell into your boathouse, the Pocock Team becomes part of your support network, upholding and supporting the standard of excellence required for success in our sport.[6]

# CHAPTER 14

---

# MANAGING THE TENSIONS OF TEAMWORK

*There was one more thing about cedar—a sort of secret that Pocock had discovered accidentally after his first shells made of the wood had been in the water for a while. . . . Once they were exposed to water both their bows and sterns tended to curve ever so slightly upward . . . because the cedar was dry when attached to the frame but then became wet after being used regularly, the wood wanted to expand slightly in length. However, the interior frame of the boat, being made of ash that remained perpetually dry and rigid, would not allow it to expand. The cedar skin thus became compressed, forcing the ends of the boat up slightly and lending it what boatbuilders called 'camber.' The result was that the boat as a whole was under subtle but continual tension like a drawn bow waiting to be released. This gave it a kind of liveliness, a tendency to spring forward on the catch of the oars in a way that no other design or material could duplicate.*

— **DANIEL JAMES BROWN**[1]

A Pocock wooden shell was built to be under continuous tension. Its performance success was tied to this tension. The same is true of successful organizations. High performance is never about just one thing. It requires managing multiple factors, often conflicting, and which must be held in ongoing dynamic tension. Organizational excellence demands a systems-based perspective placed in constructive tension managed by an emotionally healthy leader of good character.

What are the key factors that must be kept in tension? Leadership, technical competence, and organizational expertise are the three key elements of organizational excellence.

The first is leadership, which makes or breaks an organization. Too often the leader is the barrier to releasing the skills, abilities, ideas, and potential of others. His deficits are often disguised by his appeals to values-based explanations—to obtain a short-term profit or output goal he must micromanage, must admonish staff, must remain aloof. Even if this leader's goal is realized, it is only by breaking down the team and harming the organization. A virtuous leader's character, conduct, humility, selfless courage, and commitment to serve others above self must be resolute. It is paramount to achieving organizational excellence. The leader's decision to embrace these qualities in others and release this resourcefulness starts with him, and then must spread throughout the organization.

The second key element of organizational performance is technical competence. All employees must have the appropriate level of knowledge, technical proficiency, skill, experience, and training for their professions. It is safe to say that most organizations place a heavy emphasis on this element to the neglect of others. Many organizations bias the mechanical over the relational, the impersonal over the personal, to their own loss. A predictable result is high turnover and untapped potential. Organizations that value the relational not only seek technical competence, but build it, along with loyalty, integrity, and love of shared purpose.

Which brings us naturally to the third key element: organizational expertise. This requires having both an understanding of organizational dynamics, and the compassion and character to develop and encourage the best in people. The evidence for an organization with this element is trust. When a leader can inspire people and develop them into a team, they build trust. When this occurs, a leader has set the conditions for further development and success. Trust engenders confidence, commitment, and an organizational culture that is unbeatable. It is this dimension—organizational expertise demonstrated by widely-shared trust—that is typically the most lacking in an underperforming organization.

An excellent organization is one in which there is high technical competence and high organizational expertise. The key measure here is sustained excellence as all organizations will go through normal fluctuations of performance metrics. The question is whether a team or organization can learn from its mistakes and experience. That an organization has achieved values-based objectives does not predict its ability to sustain excellence. Evidence of its embrace of love, integrity, truth, excellence, and relationships will.

There is no singular, secret recipe for creating a high performance team animated by LITER. It demands a holistic approach that keeps multiple things in constant and evolving tension. To do this, a leader needs a high level of emotional intelligence. *Harvard Business Review* suggests that an effective leader must simultaneously balance seven tensions.[2]

1. **The Expert vs. the Learner**—here, technical competence needs to be balanced with relational humility. A leader must be willing to learn from others.
2. **The Constant vs. the Adaptor**—here, leaders must recognize that they are working in fast-changing environments and must be always willing to challenge the status quo.
3. **The Tactician vs. the Visionary**—here, the visionary leader must be constantly grounded in a concrete road map as to how to achieve their goal. Reality must be constantly tested.
4. **The Teller vs. the Listener**—here, the leader must value listening carefully to others before making decisions. This must be balanced with the leader's experience, ability, and viewpoint.
5. **The Power Holder vs. The Power Sharer**—here, the balance between returning authority to others and retaining authority must be balanced depending on the context of the decision and the expertise of those involved.
6. **The Intuitionist vs. the Analyst**—here, going with one's gut must be balanced with the slower approach of receiving and assessing analytic data. There are certainly times when there is no time to wait for more data and when the data cannot take into consideration all the nuances that the decision demands.

7.  **The Perfectionist vs. the Accelerator**—here, the need for the best can get in the way of good. Many key decisions must be made before perfection can be achieved, and yet hasty decisions without ample consideration can also lead to bad results.

A highly-developed emotional intelligence is what allows effective leaders to avoid rigidly adopting one approach over the other. Instead, they exhibit the ability to be ambidextrous depending on the context and people involved. To best achieve this balance, the leader will go beyond emotional intelligence and display his virtue intelligence. He will put systems in place that foster feedback and build trust. Because people, and relationships among people, are the key, leadership cannot be approached in a mechanistic style or without a team approach. Effective leadership embraces these tensions. The best way to encourage teams and organizations that are eager to navigate tensions, change, and performance is to populate them with difference-makers. These are men and women who collectively understand their individual contributions are to a higher purpose, a greater good.

People want to make a difference. People want to work within a high performing team. They want to be fully engaged in their work. They want leaders who strive for excellence. The winning edge in a racing shell is the same as that for every organization: the people in the boat. Make no mistake about it, developing an E\* organization is challenging and often messy work. It takes time and dedication. The antidote to burnout and disengagement, to selfish short-term thinking, is an emphasis on swing, or the seamless collective contribution of everyone's maximum effort to realize the optimal outcome.

Creating swing within an organization is the task and responsibility of every leader. It is an experience that, when achieved, few will ever forget. Pocock made this clear when he stated, "When you get the rhythm in an eight, it's pure pleasure to be in it. It's easy work when the rhythm comes—that is 'swing' as they call it. I've heard men shriek out with delight when the swing came in an eight; it's a thing they'll never forget as long as they live."[3]

The concept of swing retains this mysterious, spiritual ineffability. It is an experienced reality that is just beyond the easily describable. To get at it, an organization's attitude toward change is critical, maintaining the necessary tensions of teamwork, and having a clear shared picture of excellence foundational. This picture must be held in common with all the team members, embodied by the leader, and then choreographed by the leader. It is only the coach or leader who has the distanced perspective to constantly observe the whole. As such, the final accountability for achieving swing is with the leader.

Excellence is swing. It is not an act or an endpoint. It is a process of unremitting improvement, continually reaching for the stars. It is only in that journey, whether at the office, at home, or out in the world, that we can feel whole. A number of years ago the chairman of a large corporation inquired, "Almost all of my businesses are doing well. I have spent a lot of money getting them there. Is it possible for all of these businesses to go from above-average to excellent?" His corporation was technically competent, but for the most part, the people-side of the business had been neglected. There were a lot of bodies strewn along the highway on his corporation's realizing just above-average performance. A leader can drive performance, but only for so long. The time will come when the team's performance declines and people are burned out.

An excellent organization, one that achieves sustained excellence, is composed of teams, unified by a common set of core virtues and conduct, a common purpose, and an unwavering commitment to reach for the stars. It always starts with the leader. The leader sets the tone, the atmosphere for development, growth, and performance. As a leader, your integrity and authenticity are measured by your conduct, which is guided by your virtue intelligence.

Because sustained high performance depends on the spiritual qualities of swing and a leader's character exhibited in her conduct is why excellence is not a synonym for perfection or success. It can't be reduced to simply winning. Excellence is as much about how things are done as the results of the effort. Excellence is:

1. An innate and unrelenting passion within a person or an organization to continually:
   - Pursue improvement, always building upon yesterday's achievements
   - Build personal relationships and organizational mastery
   - Admit and learn from failures
   - Seek better practices and processes
   - Develop integrated and cohesive teamwork and support
   - Set high standards, holding people accountable
   - Not be satisfied with today's performance or results
   - Learn from both success and failure

2. Not about self or looking good, but about the sustained pursuit of a worthy goal, a mission, a purpose.
3. Not the endpoint of a race, but the journey of learning and growing to get there.

The journey of excellence leads to sustained, exemplary levels of performance. Evidence of excellence is quite clear. Organizations with a sustained pursuit of excellence have an engaged and highly-motivated workforce, high levels of trust, well-integrated teams, better outcomes, and a better bottom line economically, socially, and environmentally.

The journey of excellence is never complete. There are always new opportunities and challenges. When the shared purpose is big and audacious, teams and organizations are required. Others are needed for their expertise, wisdom, encouragement, and willingness to roll up their sleeves and work. When one stumbles, another can pick him up. When there is success, all can celebrate. When there is failure, all can learn and grow. The team is in it together for the long haul.

There has been much that has been written about leadership. In the end, leadership is not about the leader at all, but the team and the performance of the team under pressure over time. The measure of a virtuous leader is her ability to manage organizational tension by creating sustained technical and relational swing within an organization.

Such leaders are rare because such leaders are rarely developed. It is my belief and experience that every leader can move closer to being a virtuous leader. It begins with a personal commitment, then develops into behavioral practices, and is evident in maintaining ongoing accountability while dealing with the actual complexities of an organization. It is sustained by the organization itself.

Organizations become what they measure. Tragically, most organizations measure the wrong things. Most organizations are animated by value propositions—quarterly results, percent increases over time, improving overheads, higher profits. All of these miss the fact that effective organizations can only function with effective leadership able to form and sustain effective teams.

High performance leaders are those that can create such teams. This is evident when diverse individuals, with differing talents and personalities, are placed in high-pressure situations and remain able to function sustainably in a cohesive and coordinated manner both in terms of their technical ability and emotional connectivity. This is an organization functioning with swing.

In most organizations, leaders are only trained and rewarded for their mastery of technical competence. Moreover, few leaders are measured based on the content of their character. The virtues of love, integrity, truth, excellence, and relationships are rarely seen as necessary performance metrics. We become what we measure and, in many cases, we are measuring the wrong things.

Because virtuous leaders are the keystone to organizational and performance excellence, the path to swing begins by measuring for these leaders.

Leadership begins with you being:

- A person of character and committed to a life that is not about self but serving others

- A person with a strong sense of self—who is grounded and self-aware recognizing her strengths and weaknesses—while desiring to learn and grow
- A person with a passion for the mission and cause
- A person who listens, questions, challenges, and encourages
- A person who holds himself and others accountable
- A builder of relationships that foster the development of excellent teams
- A person who displays empathy, who seeks to understand others when their experiences and perspectives are distinctly different from her own
- A person focused on building teams and not her own career
- A person with appropriate technical expertise

Leadership begins with you, but it is not about you. Your commitment to your followers must be unwavering. This is manifested by:

- Communicating a clear vision/purpose
- Knowing your people
  - What is important to them
  - What their dreams and concerns are
  - Their strengths and needed areas for growth
  - What is needed for them to be successful
- Building their skills and abilities
  - Ensure the basics
  - Professional mastery
  - Personal development

- Setting standards of excellence
  - Holding people accountable
  - Each person knows and owns their area of responsibility
  - Developing standardized administrative and work processes
- Providing constructive feedback
  - Publicly and privately saying thank you
- Seeking their input and feedback
  - Processes and practices that can be improved or removed
  - What is going well and what is not
  - How you can help team performance

It is only after these matters are aggressively pursued that the leader's technical competence comes into play.

Finally, it should be reinforced that this is not a static check-list, but an ongoing process that can only be developed from experience over time and experience that includes crises and failure. A book can only point as a guide. It is experience that makes it real and gets leadership squarely into the bones of an individual. Leaders are not born. They are made during the daily grind. Their leadership abilities are then revealed in moments of intense competition and crisis. When this kind of leader spills over onto the entire team, the team is then set up for the experience of swing. Swing is not an accident, but the culmination of a host of variables coming into perfect harmony.

Leadership is never learned in a vacuum, through a book, or in an MBA program. It is only learned in practice. Such leaders are virtuous not because they are inherently special, but because they always make a lasting difference. They are the difference-makers.

# THE CALLING OF DIFFERENCE-MAKERS

*It's a great art, is rowing,*
*It's the finest art there is.*
*It's a symphony of motion.*
*And when you're rowing well*
*Why it's nearing perfection—*
*And when you reach perfection*
*You're touching the Divine,*
*It touches the you of you's*
*Which is your soul.*

— **GEORGE POCOCK**

There are leaders who can accomplish a task. And then there are leaders who can accomplish a task through a team. And—most rare—there are leaders who can consistently accomplish, with teams, difficult tasks demanding dedication to excellence.

These are the virtuous leaders. These are the curators of swing, the makers of meaning, and the magicians of the soul.

It is to these leaders that this book is dedicated, for they are the ultimate difference-makers.

Leaders are made, not born. The same is true of an individual's character, the virtues you exemplify, embody, encourage. An unerring marker of a leader's character are the relationships visible governing his team.

A team accomplishment far outweighs an individual accomplishment. It is greater because it is far more difficult to achieve. It is greater because it has a far wider and lasting impact. It is greater because it expands the significance of meaning from an individual to a group, a community, an organization. It is greater because it most closely resembles the collaborative ecosystem of nature. An individual can accomplish great things; a team can accomplish far greater things, always. A virtuous team evidencing the power of swing can accomplish the greatest things, visible in performance and outcomes that advance purpose and meaning that transcends the team. When they do this, it effectively reflects the Divine.

Intuitively we know this to be true. We have all brushed up against the fact that the experiences and accomplishments that matter the most in a life well-lived are relational experiences, whether enjoyed with family, friends, teammates, or colleagues. When you are part of a team—it doesn't matter the sport—that realizes its most ambitious goal articulated at the start of a season, you will recall that experience for years. When you are part of a team—it doesn't matter the organization—that exceeds every metric it set for itself at the start of the calendar year, you will recall that experience for years. A meaningful accomplishment of a team is a memory that time does not fade. Aging oarsmen and battle-scarred soldiers return for their reunions. The intensity of the comradeship forged in competition, like comradeship forged on the battlefield, never fades. When you have "touched the Divine" together it touches the depths of your soul.

The lines that open this last chapter are George Yeoman Pocock's rowing creed. Fittingly, when Pocock died in Seattle on March 19, 1976, four days short of his eighty-fifth birthday, they were the closing words of his memorial services at the University Christian Church. In multiple endeavors, working with multiple teams, Pocock had repeatedly achieved swing. He had lived a life touching the Divine.

Organizations become what they measure. So, too, do people. The most important thing to measure is the most difficult thing to measure. For leaders, it is their character defined by their deliberate and effortful adherence to transcendent virtues. For organizations, it is the ineffable experience of swing in their teams.

There is no fixed yardstick or formula to measure character or swing because every situation is different, and every team is composed of different kinds of people. Nonetheless, organizations will not achieve swing unless they aspire to swing. Mentoring that aspiration in a team is the true measure of a high performing leader. This demands holistic relational thinking. Make attaining swing the team's ambition and the priorities of an organization change. Attaining swing demands placing the team above the individual. It can require highlighting the soft skills of empathy and listening. Swing manifests when the balance of character and conduct of each team member is in service to the emotional and virtue intelligence of every team member. Swing is the collective experience to which all high performing teams aspire. It is also the haunted longing of every employee. Every team member longs for the additive experience of flow with others toward a shared goal of noble accomplishment. Swing is relational poetry under pressure, the ballet of achievement forged in adversity.

Swing is possible only when it is built on the foundation of the five transcendent virtues of love, integrity, truth, excellence, and relationships. That is the promise at the center of the virtue proposition. Its practices, its models, its moral compass point to a new way forward for high performance leaders who intend to lead teams to extraordinary success. It is also the answer to our crisis of leadership. It starts with the virtue proposition. You are invited to take up the calling and make a difference.

# ENDNOTES

## Introduction

1    Jim C. Rahn, "For Such a Time as This," The Jubilee Centre's 10th Anniversary Conference, Oriel College, Oxford, September 8, 2022: https://www.jubileecentre.ac.uk/userfiles/jubileecentre/pdf/Rahn-pdf.pdf/.

2    James Davison Hunter, *The Death of Character: Moral Education in an Age Without Good or Evil* (Basic Books, 2000), p. xv.

3    James L. Nolan, Jr. *The Therapeutic State: Justifying Government at Century's End* (New York University Press, 1998), pgs. 2, 3.

4    Steven Zaillian, *Schindler's List Screenplay*: https://static1.squarespace.com/static/5a1c2452268b96d901cd3471/t/5ba9a79cb208fc63480cff81/1537845149013/schindlers-list-screenplay-by-steven-zaillian.pdf/.

5    Aristotle, *The Metaphysics* (Penguin Classics, 1999), 8.6, p. 231.

6    Sted Garber, e-mail message to author, October 20, 2021. Sted Garber was a varsity oarsman at Navy from 1962-1965.

7    Jon R. Katzenbach and Douglas K. Smith, *The Wisdom of Teams: Creating the High-Performance Organization* (HarperBusiness Book, 1999), p. xvi.

8    Gordon Newell and Dick Erickson, *Ready All! George Yeoman Pocock and Crew Racing* (University of Washington Press, 1987), p. 144.

9    Daniel James Brown, *The Boys in the Boat: Nine Americans and Their Epic Quest for Gold at the 1936 Berlin Olympics* (Penguin Books 2013), p. 179.

10   Ibid., p. 353.

# Chapter 1

1   Gordon Newell and Dick Erickson, *Ready All! George Yeoman Pocock and Crew Racing* (University of Washington Press, 1987), p. 85.

2   Seth Godin, "All the Answers": https://seths.blog/2021/09/all-the-answers/.

3   EEOC Releases Fiscal Year 2019 Enforcement and Litigation Data: https://www.eeoc.gov/newsroom/eeoc-releases-fiscal-year-2019-enforcement-and-litigation-data/.

4   Clayton M. Christensen, "How Will You Measure Your Life: Don't Reserve Your Best Business Thinking for Your Career," *Harvard Business Review,* July-August 2010, p. 18.

# Chapter 2

1   Gordon Newell and Dick Erickson, *Ready All! George Yeoman Pocock and Crew Racing* (University of Washington Press, 1987), p. 84.

2   Annie Dillard, *The Writing Life* (Harper Perennial, 2013): https://www.themarginalian.org/2013/06/07/annie-dillard-the-writing-life-1/.

3   David Brooks, *The Road to Character* (Random House, 2015), p. xi.

4   World Association of Nuclear Operators (WANO), "Our Mission", https://www.wano.info/about-us/our-mission.

5   Clayton M. Christensen, "How Will You Measure Your Life," p. 16.

6   C.S. Lewis, *The Abolition of Man* (The Macmillan Company, 1971), p. 29.

7   Gerald Zaltman, *How Customer's Think: Essential Insights into the Mind of the Market* (Harvard Business School Publishing, 2003). See also Daniel Kahneman, *Thinking, Fast and Slow* (Farrar, Straus, and Giroux, 2011).

# Chapter 3

1   Daniel James Brown, *The Boys in the Boat: Nine Americans and Their Epic Quest for Gold at the 1936 Berlin Olympics* (Penguin Books 2013), p. 215.

2   Ibid., p. 213.

3   Ibid., p. 214.

4   Andy Crouch, *Strong and Weak: Embracing a Life of Love, Risk, and True Flourishing* (InterVarsity Press, 2002).

5   Steven B. Sample, *The Contrarian's Guide to Leadership* (Jossey-Bass, 2003).

## Chapter 4

1  Daniel James Brown, *The Boys in the Boat: Nine Americans and Their Epic Quest for Gold at the 1936 Berlin Olympics* (Penguin Books 2013), p. 231.
2  Ibid., p. 343-351.
3  Ibid., p. 347.

## Chapter 5

1  Gordon Newell and Dick Erickson, *Ready All! George Yeoman Pocock and Crew Racing* (University of Washington Press, 1987), p. 82.
2  Robert K. Greenleaf, *Servant Leadership: A Journey into the Nature of Legitimate Power and Greatness* (Paulist Press, 2002). See also https://www.greenleaf.org/what-is-servant-leadership/.
3  C. S. Lewis, *The Abolition of Man* (The Macmillan Company, 1971), p. 29.
4  "I fear for the future of the West if it loses its faith. You cannot defend Western freedom on the basis of moral relativism, the only morality left when we lose our mooring in a sacred ontology or a divine-human covenant. No secular morality withstood Nazi Germany or Stalinist Russia. No secular morality today has the force to withstand the sustained onslaught of ruthless religious extremism. Neither market economics nor liberal democracy has the power, in and of itself, to inspire people to make sacrifices for the common good." Jonathan Sacks, *The Great Partnership: Science, Religion, and the Search for Meaning* (Schocken, 2012), p. 109.
5  Jonathan Sacks, *Celebrating Life* (Bloomsbury, 2019), p. 54.
6  Marcus Aurelius, *Meditations* (Penguin Classics, 2006), Book 3, Section 5.
7  Jonathan Sacks, *The Home We Build Together: Recreating Society* (Bloomsbury Continuum, 2009), p. 240.

## Chapter 6

1  Daniel James Brown, *The Boys in the Boat: Nine Americans and Their Epic Quest for Gold at the 1936 Berlin Olympics* (Penguin Books 2013), p. 48.
2  Daniel Goleman, *Emotional Intelligence: Why It Can Matter More than IQ* (Random House, 2005).
3  Steven J. Stein and Howard E. Book, *The EQ Edge: Emotional Intelligence and Your Success* (Jossey-Bass, 2010), p. 17.
4  Ibid., p. 20.

5    Hile Rutledge and Sigval Berg, *EQ Workbook – An Interpretation and Application Guide to Emotional Intelligence and the EQ-i.* (Severn Leadership Group, 2020). It should be noted that Hile Rutledge is president of Otto Kroeger Associates (OKA). OKA is recognized as the leading U.S. training center for EQ-i2.0.

6    Daniel James Brown, *The Boys in the Boat: Nine Americans and Their Epic Quest for Gold at the 1936 Berlin Olympics* (Penguin Books 2013), p. 283.

7    Steven J. Stein and Howard E. Book, *The EQ Edge: Emotional Intelligence and Your Success* (Jossey-Bass, 2010), p. 289.

## Chapter 7

1    Daniel James Brown, *The Boys in the Boat: Nine Americans and Their Epic Quest for Gold at the 1936 Berlin Olympics* (Penguin Books 2013), p. 36.

2    Joseph Luft and Harry Ingham, "The Johari Window Model": https://www.communicationtheory.org/the-johari-window-model/.

3    Brené Brown, "The Power of Vulnerability": https://www.ted.com/talks/brene_brown_the_power_of_vulnerability/.

4    Daniel James Brown, *The Boys in the Boat: Nine Americans and Their Epic Quest for Gold at the 1936 Berlin Olympics* (Penguin Books 2013), p. 55.

5    Ibid., p. 78.

## Chapter 8

1    Ibid., p. 179.

2    Euripides, *Euripides IV: Helen, The Phoenician Women, Orestes* (University of Chicago Press, 2013), Fragment 809.

3    Seth Godin, "Perfect; Could Be Better": https://seths.blog/2016/04/perfect-could-be-better/.

4    Ron Carucci, "How to Actually Encourage Employee Accountability," *Harvard Business Review,* November 23, 2020: https://hbr.org/2020/11/how-to-actually-encourage-employee-accountability/.

5    Gallup Survey, "State of the Global Workplace 2023 Report: The Voice of the World's Employees": file:///Users/djsjr/Downloads/state-of-the-global-workplace-2023-download.pdf/.

6    Paul Oestreicher, *Camelot, Inc.: Leadership and Management Insights from King Arthur and the Round Table* (Holtzbrinck, 2011).

7    Rebecca Knight, "How to Give Your Team Feedback," *Harvard Business Review,* June 16, 2014: https://hbr.org/2014/06/how-to-give-your-team-feedback/.

8    Muriel Wilkins, "Signs You Are a Micromanager," *Harvard Business Review,* November 11, 2014: https://hbr.org/2014/11/signs-that-youre-a-micromanager/.

## Chapter 9

1    Daniel James Brown, *The Boys in the Boat: Nine Americans and Their Epic Quest for Gold at the 1936 Berlin Olympics* (Penguin Books 2013), p. 353.

2    Rob Goffee and Gareth Jones, *The Character of a Corporation: How Your Company's Culture Can Make or Break Your Business* (HarperBusiness, 1998).

3    Gordon Newell and Dick Erickson, *Ready All! George Yeoman Pocock and Crew Racing* (University of Washington Press, 1987), p. 158.

4    Daniel James Brown, *The Boys in the Boat: Nine Americans and Their Epic Quest for Gold at the 1936 Berlin Olympics* (Penguin Books 2013), p. 229.

## Chapter 10

1    Lao Tzu: https://www.brainyquote.com/quotes/lao_tzu_151133/.

2    John A. Byrne, Business Week, 3636-3644 (McGraw-Hill, 1999), p.54.

3    David Burnham, "InterActive Leadership," Burnham Rosen Group.

## Chapter 11

1    Daniel James Brown, *The Boys in the Boat: Nine Americans and Their Epic Quest for Gold at the 1936 Berlin Olympics* (Penguin Books 2013), p. 357.

2    Ibid., p. 283.

3    C. S. Lewis, *The Best of C.S. Lewis* (Christianity Today, 1969), p. 100.

4    Clayton M. Christensen, "How Will You Measure Your Life," p. 19.

5    Daniel James Brown, *The Boys in the Boat: Nine Americans and Their Epic Quest for Gold at the 1936 Berlin Olympics* (Penguin Books 2013), p. 335.

## Chapter 12

1    Ibid., p. 352.

2    Ibid., p. 185.

3    Gordon Newell and Dick Erickson, *Ready All! George Yeoman Pocock and Crew Racing* (University of Washington Press, 1987), p. 133.

4    Kim Scott, "Small Talk Is an Overrated Way to Build Relationships with Your Employees," *Harvard Business Review,* July 25, 2017: https://hbr.org/2017/07/small-talk-is-an-overrated-way-to-build-relationships-with-your-employees/.

5    Jamie Dimon, "The ABCs of Decay": https://valuetainment.com/jaime-dimon-warning-about-recession-abcs-of-decay/.

6    Roger Schwartz, *Smart Leaders, Smarter Teams: How You and Your Team Get Unstuck to Get Results* (Jossey-Bass, 2013) in Rebecca Knight, "How to Give Your Team Feedback," *Harvard Business Review,* June 16, 2014: https://hbr.org/2014/06/how-to-give-your-team-feedback/.

7    Gordon Newell and Dick Erickson, *Ready All! George Yeoman Pocock and Crew Racing* (University of Washington Press, 1987), p. 139.

8    Ibid., p.151.

9    David John Seel, Jr., *Network Power: The Science of Making a Difference* (Whithorn Press, 2021).

## Chapter 13

1    Https://www.pocock.com/.

2    Gordon Newell and Dick Erickson, *Ready All! George Yeoman Pocock and Crew Racing* (University of Washington Press, 1987), p. 62.

3    Edgar H. Schein and Peter A. Schein, *The Corporate Culture Survival Guide* (Wiley, 2019), John P. Kotter, *Leading Change* (Harvard Business Review Press, 2012), Clayton M. Christensen, Matt Marx, and Howard H. Stevenson, "The Tools of Cooperation and Change," *Harvard Business Review,* October 2006: https://hbr.org/2006/10/the-tools-of-cooperation-and-change/.

4    John P. Kotter, *Leading Change* (Harvard Business Review Press, 2012), p. 59.

5    Elizabeth Kubler-Ross, *On Death and Dying* (Scribner, 2014).

6    "Building the World's Finest Racing Shells," Pocock, accessed July 31, 2023, https://www.pocock.com.

## Chapter 14

1    Daniel James Brown, *The Boys in the Boat: Nine Americans and Their Epic Quest for Gold at the 1936 Berlin Olympics* (Penguin Books 2013), p. 139.

2    Jennifer Jordan, Michael Wade, and Elizabeth Teracino, "Every Leader Needs to Navigate These Seven Tensions," *Harvard Business Review,* February 20, 2020: https://hbr.org/2020/02/every-leader-needs-to-navigate-these-7-tensions/.

3    Gordon Newell and Dick Erickson, *Ready All! George Yeoman Pocock and Crew Racing* (University of Washington Press, 1987), p. 159.

# ACKNOWLEDGMENTS

I am enormously grateful for teachers, mentors, colleagues, and friends who have been willing to listen, question, challenge, and encourage me. Without them, my life's journey would have been much different. I would like to acknowledge Martha Berg, Kristen Logan, Suzanne Lieuwen, Sarah Berg, Bill and Trudy Nies, Jonas Segal, Fred Meuser, Dave Shugert, Zack Pate, Matt Carr, and the communities of faith of which Martha and I have been a part.

I am also grateful for all the encouragement, support, and advice I have received in writing *The Virtue Proposition*. In many ways this book has been a team effort. I would like to thank Thomas LeBien of Moon and Company for skillfully guiding me through the writing of this book; John Seel for significant insight into networks and virtues; Hile Rutledge for his collaboration on emotional intelligence and associated behaviors; Julie Campbell, Judy Farrell, Ted and Anne Parker, Ray Rottman, Dwight Holloway, Hal Chappelear, Kathleen Morrison, Ray Steinmetz, Terry Benedict, Sted Garber, John McGaha, and the Severn Leadership Group (SLG) team for their tireless effort in translating this book into action and changing lives.

# ABOUT THE AUTHOR

Sig Berg is the founder of The Severn Leadership Group in Annapolis, Maryland. A distinguished graduate of the U.S. Naval Academy, he served as the chief engineer on the nuclear-powered submarine USS *Sunfish* (SSN 649). Berg completed the Advanced Management Program at the Harvard Graduate School of Business and has a master of divinity degree from Trinity Lutheran Seminary. He was an executive vice president at the Institute of Nuclear Power Operations and managing director of the World Association of Nuclear Operators in London and the senior vice president for Infrastructure Development and Training at UniStar Nuclear Energy. Berg also served as a senior pastor at Good Shepherd Church in Naperville, Illinois, over a congregation of nearly 1,000 members. He and his wife, Martha, live in Annapolis, Maryland. He has three daughters and six grandchildren.

# ABOUT SEVERN
# LEADERSHIP GROUP

The Severn Leadership Group (SLG) fosters a better world by developing and supporting virtuous leaders and teams to be agents of transformational change. For over a decade, the SLG has influenced the character of leadership across a variety of industries, government, and the armed forces. SLG leaders and followers have a track record of catalyzing transcendent, virtuous team cultures that accelerate team performance and multiply their impact. More information about the Severn Leadership Group can be found at severnleadership.org.